P9-DML-361
LIVING LIKE ED

ED BEGLEY, JR.

Clarkson Potter/Publishers
New York

This book is printed on
100% postconsumer recycled paper.

Published in the United States by Clarkson
Potter/Publishers, an imprint of the Crown Publishing
Group, a division of Random House, Inc., New York.
www.crownpublishing.com
www.clarksonpotter.com

Library of Congress Cataloging-in-Publication Data
Begley, Ed.
Living like Ed / Ed Begley, Jr.
1. Green movement. 2. Environmental responsibility.
I. Title.
GE195.7.B44 2008
333.72—dc22 2007038921
978-0-307-39643-3
Printed in the United States of America
Design by Lauren Monchik
Photographs: BCII-Jennifer Shields
10 9 8 7 6 5 4 3 2
First Edition

To my family—my wife, Rachelle,
my son, Nicholas, and my daughters,
Amanda and Hayden—and to
Bruno Kirby and Ingrid Begley

GE kVs
Watthour Electricity Meter
21 337 298
CITY OF LOS ANGELES
ND9–1110151
USA
Single Phase
CL 200 240V 3W FM2S
60Hz TA 30 Kh 7.2
R9G0703 104692

CONTENTS

HOL

FOREWORD
BY RACHELLE CARSON-BEGLEY

Years ago, I came to Hollywood to follow my dreams, fall in love, become an actress, and live like a queen.

Well, I am an actress and I did fall in love with my prince, Ed Begley, Jr. And now we're married and I'm living like . . . well, what exactly am I living like? Certainly not the Hollywood royalty of my fantasies.

Yes, my husband's a star, but he's decided we won't live in Beverly Hills. Instead we have a charming little house in Studio City, complete with a white picket fence made entirely of recycled plastic milk jugs. We have a fleet of sporty vehicles: his electric car, my hybrid, and our bicycles.

All of the power for our house is produced on-site. Solar panels pretty much cover the roof, and we have our very own wind turbine.

It's not quite the palace I imagined as a girl growing up in Atlanta. But let's face it: I married into a lifestyle.

I like to joke that before I met Ed, I drove a Hummer, but the truth is I've always been interested in the environment. My dad had a little farm, and we always had fresh fruit and vegetables. As a child, I would scream "Polluters!" out of the car window at big trucks. And I do remember that when the Chattahoochee River turned blue, and it was not a blue you'd see in nature, I thought, "This is not right."

So I always had a degree of environmental awareness.

On the other hand, I like fashion. I like nice cars and beautiful homes. I like good food. And while I had always appreciated other people's dedication to environmental causes, it wasn't my big thing. I just didn't have a lot of patience for people who had holier-than-thou attitudes about saving the planet. So when Ed and I started going out, I liked to be sort of provocative with Hollywood types who made a big deal of their environmentalism. On our second or third date, a double date with Don Henley and his now wife, I said something like, "So what's the deal with the environment? There are so many other issues out there. There are children's issues. There are women's issues. There are people dying all over the planet. It seems pretty easy to be into the environment. It's sort of a safe cause."

And Don said, "Without the environment, we'd be without the basic human rights of clean air and fresh water." He made a good point.

But it wasn't until Ed and I really got serious that my lifestyle began to change in a big way.

That's not to say it's been an easy transition. Where Ed sees only the environment—and the financial savings—I can see the other side. I care about the environment, I really do, but I also care about aesthetics. I help our family find some sort of balance.

In this book, I speak for the "average guy," the one who can't always remember which kind of plastic can go into the recycling bin—or who can't understand why a rain barrel has to be big and orange and ugly. Surely there must be an attractive rain barrel out there someplace! Just as, surely, there must be organic clothing that's flattering and stylish and comfortable, too.

One thing I've gotta admit: You can't accuse Ed of "going green" to be chic or because everyone else around him is doing it. He doesn't go whichever way the wind blows. He's not a faddist. He doesn't follow the trends.

In 1990 it wasn't trendy to ride a bike for any other purpose than to get fit. No one did it to preserve the environment—or to stay out of a gasoline-powered car—unless they were a granola-head in Humboldt County. In fact, eco-consciousness was so far under the radar at that time that Ed's environmental efforts were seen as weird. As his wife, it's been hard to stand by and watch people treat Ed like some kind of green freak.

I think it even cost Ed a little bit in his career. His actions made some people feel uncomfortable or like he was judging them. He's never been one to judge; he just did what heroes do: He made a sacrifice for something bigger than himself.

But now the attitudes are shifting. There are lots of like-minded people in Hollywood who think, "I like Ed's commitment to the environment; he's really a good guy. Wouldn't it be funny to cast him as the masked murderer in this show?"

That's the great thing about "hard work finally meets opportunity"—now everyone's eager to hear what he has to say because it's become more chic, but he's just saying what he believes and has believed in for more than three decades. And at least no one's making fun of him anymore!

I'm glad to see that the focus on the environment has grown to include my biggest causes, too: women's and children's health. The health of the environment obviously affects every one of us every single day. What do we feed our children and ourselves? What do we wear? What do we breathe? Is there poison in the air? On our skin? In our food? I know I take it personally, and I hope you will, too. After all, if I can learn to accept and live with and even embrace the lifestyle changes that living with Ed have brought into my world, I bet you can start living like Ed, too. And we'll all be just a little bit better for it.

RadioShack
LIGHT

INTRODUCTION

A big environmental bandwagon has been rolling through town lately, and a lot of folks inside and outside of Hollywood have hopped on. And I couldn't be happier! Though sadly it's taken some pretty dire environmental predictions to focus everyone's attention on the harm we are doing to the planet, I believe the message is finally being heard and that more people every day are looking around to see what they can do to live in a more eco-friendly, responsible way. Fortunately, there's a lot that every single one of us can do. In a nutshell, *I believe we need to live simply so that others can simply live.* And I'm here to show you how.

People who know me as an actor may not realize that I've got another passion that's at least as important to me: the environment. Sometimes, when people see me at a grocery store or at a farmers' market selling my Begley's Best nontoxic cleaning supplies, they're kind of baffled, wondering if I've fallen on hard times. It's surely a surprise, after seeing me on TV or in movies, to find me standing there hawking cleaning products.

Actually, I still work quite regularly as an actor. But I also make time to sell these nontoxic cleaning supplies—and I put my name on them—because I really believe in them. And if you've ever seen my television show, *Living with Ed,* about how my wife, Rachelle, and our daughter, Hayden, and I live, you know my commitment to living simply, cleanly, and efficiently doesn't stop there.

I got involved with the environment in 1970, the year the first Earth Day was held. I started recycling, composting, and buying biodegradable soaps and detergents, and I bought my first electric car.

In 1990 I bought a little house that had been built in 1936, long before the phrase *energy efficiency* was common parlance. I thought, "I've been a quote/unquote environmentalist for twenty years now. It's time for me to go a little further." I had a book, *50 Simple Ways to Save the Earth.* I thought, "Let me try all fifty," figuring maybe half of them would work.

Well, guess what? They *all* worked. Every last one. Some of the results were subtle, but most were not. I saved energy, and I saved dollars.

It's been nearly forty years since I took those first small steps. And now I'm ready to share what I've learned with you. I'll start with some of the easy things you can do in your home. Some of these changes are simple. They just require you to establish a new habit. Others involve making a purchase, such as drapes or even a new dishwasher. You may want to make a few of the changes or, like I did, try to implement them all. Either way, I promise you the results will be concrete and they will be worth the effort, both to the environment and to your bottom line. And if that's the case, where is the downside, right?

Since I first started down this path, I've made *many* changes in my life. Actually, I've used myself as a guinea pig a lot of the time. I've tried things like producing solar electricity for my home, driving an electric car, and cooking in a solar oven. I've found ways to reduce the amount of trash I produce, ways to reduce the amount of electricity and water that I use, and ways to grow my own food.

This book is designed to help you learn from my experience. After thirty-eight years of doing this, I know what works. I know what saves energy, what saves water—and what saves money! So maybe you can use my life as an example of one way to take this journey.

Of course I don't expect you to make *all* these changes right off the bat. It's really a process. I've gone pretty far with this stuff, but you might want to start out small. Either way, I'll show you a lot of things you can do, from changing the kind of lightbulbs you buy or shopping for organic produce at your local farmers' market to purchasing a new appliance or vehicle.

The simple fact is, you don't climb Mount Everest in a single day. First you climb up to base camp. Then you stop there and you get acclimated for a while. After you've adjusted to the altitude, *then* you take the next step and climb a little higher. And then you stop again and get acclimated. And you only climb as high as you are able at each stage.

Becoming environmentally aware—and adjusting your lifestyle to reflect your beliefs and your values—is the same kind of process. You take a small step and you prove to yourself that you can do it. You compare your electric bills and you see that the change you made was good for your wallet. You see how much money you saved and you see how little it affected the quality of your life. In fact, I'll bet you barely even notice the difference.

When you feel more confident and more comfortable—better acclimated, if you will—you make one or two more changes, and so on and so on.

Six Areas of Your Life

There's a certain fear factor about "going green." Many reasonable people think, "Wait a minute. I don't wanna be shivering in the dark, just so I can save a little energy."

But that's not what it's about. You'll still be able to have a cool beverage and a warm shower. I'm just gonna show you how to have those things more efficiently.

I sometimes refer to my house as the SS *Begley*, and Rachelle claims that I run it like I'm the captain of a ship. But it's all about efficiency, organization, maintenance, and conservation. And my house is just one area of my life where I've applied these principles.

My goal is to help you understand the choices you can make to simplify your life, to help the environment, to save energy, and to save money. In the pages that follow I'll offer suggestions for all six of the areas in our lives where we can be more efficient:

- home
- transportation
- recycling
- energy
- garden and kitchen
- clothing and hair and skin care

Anyone who takes a step toward helping the environment makes me happy. I see people—even big businesses—making progress all the time. It doesn't matter if it's Wal-Mart or McDonald's or one of my friends or neighbors. In the 10k of life, when a runner who seems to have been lagging behind sprints ahead, he deserves a pat on the back and assistance in the race.

I'll help you discover some of the changes, large and small, that you can make. I've even marked these suggestions to make them easy to spot.

EASY CHANGES. These are the low-hanging fruit. These are changes you can make almost effortlessly and at little or no expense—in fact, some may even save you money right off the bat! And virtually all of them will end up saving you money in the long term. These changes are noted with a symbol like the one at the left.

NOT-SO-BIG CHANGES. These changes will cost you anywhere from $50 to just under $500 to implement, but while they require a bit more of a financial investment, each has a real, quantifiable payoff. You can spot these changes wherever you see this symbol.

BIG CHANGES. Not surprisingly, some of the biggest payoffs require the biggest up-front investment. You may not be able to make a lot of these changes right away, but it's worth knowing what they are as well as their benefits so you can make the best choices when it comes to replacing big-ticket items or doing significant work on your home. You can find these changes wherever you see this symbol.

Forward (and Onward)

I'm happy to report that I've seen a lot of progress since I first started on my own personal green campaign. In 1970 the air quality in Los Angeles was atrocious. You know how they have snow days back east? Well, in L.A., we had smog days, days when the air quality was so bad, children were told not to go to school!

Since then, the number of cars in the L.A. basin has quadrupled as the population and number of multicar households have grown. But you know what? The air quality has not gotten worse. It hasn't even stayed the same.

It's gotten *better.* We've got four times the cars and half the ozone. That's really good.

That's been over the course of nearly forty years, during a period when most people hadn't even *started* thinking about how their actions might affect the environment. Imagine how much of a difference we can make in the *next* forty years, as people like you read this book and make just one or two or ten of the changes. Because this is a fight we can win in stages. Together, we can all get to the top of Mount Everest. Start with the low-hanging fruit, move on to the more significant changes, and before you know it, you'll be living just like me.

HOME

TAKING AN OLD HOME AND MAKING IT GREEN

1

I bought our house in 1988, a simple little two-bedroom house on a small lot in Studio City, California. Given my financial position at the time, it was a great move that has also turned out to be great for my career—I've never felt pressured to take a role I didn't love just so I could make a huge mortgage payment. Of course, by Hollywood standards, this house is a shack. But by world standards, as I'm sure you know, it is a palace.

Retrofitting an Old House vs. Building New

Few of us have the resources to build a more energy-efficient house from the ground up. I didn't have the money to do that, and I didn't have the will to do that. Plus I *liked* my house.

So, I set out to make my home as environmentally sound as I could in every aspect. I knew that with insulation, a drought-tolerant garden, double-pane windows, an energy-saving thermostat, and solar panels I eventually put on the roof, I could make this a much more efficient structure.

Indeed, by the time I was done, I had made my home nearly as energy efficient as a new one. And you can do the same for your home, wherever you live.

The key to saving energy in your home is *controlling* energy use. Clearly, there are many ways to do this, from simple changes in what you do and how you do it to more-intense home improvement projects. Because so much of the energy used in your home is used to keep it warm in the winter and cool in the summer, we'll start with ways you can control your heating and cooling needs.

And there's another important point I want to mention right up front: You don't have to *own* your home to make many of these changes. There's a lot you can do even if you're renting, or if you own a condominium or another type of structure where you might be limited as to the kinds of changes you can make.

So why bother making these changes? Because they'll make your home more energy efficient, which means you'll be helping the environment by saving natural resources. It also means you'll be helping yourself and saving money—sometimes really big money. So no matter where you live right now, you can make some changes that will make a real difference.

A Fresh Filter

Perhaps the easiest thing you can do today is change the air filter for your heating and air-conditioning system. Many people think, "Filter? There's a filter?" If that's you, yours

Keeping your air filter clean can reduce an air conditioner's energy consumption a lot—by as

probably hasn't been changed in a while.

Most central heating and air-conditioning systems have a filter at the air intake—on a wall or on the ceiling—and many window and wall-unit air conditioners have a filter element on the front that needs to be changed, too.

I change mine regularly, sometimes six times a year, because we have two cats and a dog, and pet hair is always blowing around. I check the air inlet for my heating and air-conditioning system regularly and often realize, "Whoa! It's time to change this thing again."

I usually change my air filter every other month.

Why is changing the filter so important? Because when the filter gets dusty or dirty or clogged, it's harder for your system to pull air through it. That means your system has to work harder, and it has to stay on longer in order to do the same amount of work.

So changing that filter regularly is the low-hanging fruit that you can pick right away. And it doesn't matter if you have central heat and air or a window- or wall-mount air conditioner. Changing the filter is a great way to make your home more energy efficient.

Beyond that, changing the filter will help if anyone in your family suffers from allergies. You can even go a step further and choose an air filter that's designed especially to trap allergens. If odors are a problem in your home, there are filters designed to trap them, too.

much as 5 to 15 percent. As much as half of the energy used in your home goes toward

An Energy-Saving Thermostat

Once you've got the air moving more efficiently through your heating and cooling system, think about how you regulate the temperature of that air.

It requires a huge amount of energy—energy that you pay for in the form of your electric, oil, or gas bills—to raise or lower the heat of your home by even a few degrees. Controlling these costs, and the amount of energy you use, means controlling the temperature both when you're at home *and* when you're away. This is the magic of an energy-saving thermostat.

Most people simply turn their heating and air-conditioning system on and off when they want to be warmer or colder. Some even leave the system on when they leave the house, so that it will be the right temperature when they return. Maybe you leave the heat running at your preferred temperature all night long—even though you're sleeping under a blanket or a comforter—because you want the house to be nice and warm when you get up in the morning.

But why spend all that money, and waste all that energy, keeping your house comfortable when you're not there, or when you can simply add another blanket to your bed at night?

If you have central heating or central air-conditioning or both, you can install and use a programmable thermostat instead of an old "set the temperature and it's either on or off" thermostat. This way, you can save energy and money *and* have your house at the right temperature when you get home, when you wake up in the morning, *and* when you're asleep.

Programming the thermostat is easy—and a real money-saver.

heating and cooling it. If you can reach a compromise in your home, a great way to save

You will have to invest some money up front; an energy-saving thermostat starts at about $65. But it will pay for itself in heating and cooling savings in a year or less if you use all of its features.

Programming Your New Thermostat

- Make sure you program the energy-saving thermostat to shut down the heat or air-conditioning automatically when you leave for work or for school, and to turn it back on 20 to 30 minutes before you expect to return.
- You'll also want to program the thermostat to reduce the temperature when you're heating the house (or to increase the temperature when you're cooling it) about 30 to 60 minutes after you normally turn in for the night. Once you're under the covers and asleep, you won't require as much heating or even cooling. (You'd be surprised how much less cooling is necessary to keep you comfortable at night. And you can always open a window in the summer if it's cooler outside at night.) Again, you just program the thermostat to return to "awake" mode 20 to 30 minutes before your alarm goes off in the morning.
- You don't need to worry about being uncomfortable if you're home all day on the weekend, either. Energy-saving thermostats let you program different settings for weekdays and weekends.
- If you plan on going out of town, make sure you override your normal programming and shut down everything until you return. The caveat here is that if you're in a very cold climate and you're worried about your pipes freezing, don't let the temp fall below 55 degrees Fahrenheit. And you might not want to shut the system down completely if you're leaving pets in your home. Even so, you can see there's tremendous potential for energy savings here.

Temperatures change day to day, so don't be afraid to adjust your program settings, daily if need be, to maximize the efficiency of your system. I check mine every time I leave the house.

energy *and* save money is to dial back your normal settings 5 to 8 degrees, then put on a

RACHELLE'S TURN

Ed used to make me crazy with that programmable thermostat. He was always tinkering with it, making us late before we'd go anywhere. And if I adjusted it myself, he was always asking, "What happened? Who touched this?" He always knew if I'd cranked the heat up a degree or two, but he kept the house bordering on freezing in the winter!

But I guess it's like anything. You can get used to wearing a sweater inside, especially when you see the difference in the energy bill. And it does make sense to save energy when we're not home. Of course, he's got that thermostat programmed to dial the heat way back at night, but I have to admit I don't mind putting an extra blanket on the bed anymore. It's not such a bad trade. With what we save on the electric bill, I get to buy more shoes!

Choosing a Comfortable Temperature

It's one thing to talk about programming the thermostat. Everybody says, "Sure, makes sense." It's another thing entirely to try to reach an agreement with the people living in your home about what temperature is comfortable.

Let me talk about the temperature in my house *before* Rachelle and *after* Rachelle. When I was single, I would keep the house at 65 to 68 degrees in the winter and 78 in the summer. I didn't think twice about simply wearing a sweater or sweatshirt in the winter and changing into a cotton T-shirt and shorts in the summer.

There is no amount of thermostat programming that can replace good ol' shutting down the heating and cooling completely when the temperatures outside and inside your home are within your own personal comfort zone. Well, that ain't gonna fly anymore in my home. I have a wife and a daughter who require considerably more creature comfort than I did when living on my own.

sweater in the winter or wear shorts in the summer. In some parts of the country, you can cut

If you have a really old heating and air-conditioning unit, you might want to consider purchasing a new Energy Star system. It's going to be a big investment, but you're going to make that money back in a few years because the units are so much more efficient now, and use so much less power. The compressors are more efficient, the fans are more efficient, everything about the system's more efficient. You can literally save up to 20 percent on your yearly heating and cooling costs with a new, more energy-efficient unit.

What Energy Star Means

Many people think Energy Star is a brand name or a particular company. Actually, it's a program created jointly by the U.S. Environmental Protection Agency and the U.S. Department of Energy. Its goal is laudable: to help everybody save money and protect the environment through energy-efficient products and practices. And the program is working.

To benefit from this program, you just look for the Energy Star symbol on a product. It's like a seal of approval. To wear it, that product has to meet strict energy efficiency guidelines.

You can find the Energy Star symbol on all kinds of things, from complete homes to appliances and office equipment, including

- central air-conditioning units and room air conditioners
- ceiling fans (another great way to reduce cooling costs and energy use)
- furnaces
- dehumidifiers
- refrigerators and freezers
- clothes washers
- dishwashers
- windows and skylights
- doors
- roofing products
- insulation

your energy bill 30 percent in the winter by going from 72 to 68 degrees. **In 2006 alone, the**

- televisions, VCRs, and DVD players
- computers and monitors
- fax machines, printers, and scanners
- cordless phones
- lighting fixtures

Purchasing Energy Star–qualified products can even get you a tax break. To find out which products qualify and which forms you'll need to submit to the Internal Revenue Service, visit the Energy Star website at www.energystar.gov.

Energy-Efficient Refrigerators

How much of a difference does it make to switch to an Energy Star–qualified product? It depends on the product. It can range from a little to a very significant difference. Say you're thinking about replacing an old refrigerator with a newer model.

Replacing your refrigerator bought in 1990 with a newer, more energy-efficient model would save enough energy to light the average household for nearly four months.

In a typical household, that fridge is the single biggest energy-consuming appliance in the kitchen. In fact, the refrigerator actually uses 25 percent of the energy consumed in most homes.

But even if you can't replace your current refrigerator, you can still help the one you've got use less energy. First, position your fridge so it's not near a heat source, which makes the fridge work harder to stay cool. You don't want it right next to the oven or right next to the dishwasher or even in the path of direct sunlight from a window.

Energy Star program saved consumers $14 billion on their utility bills. According to the

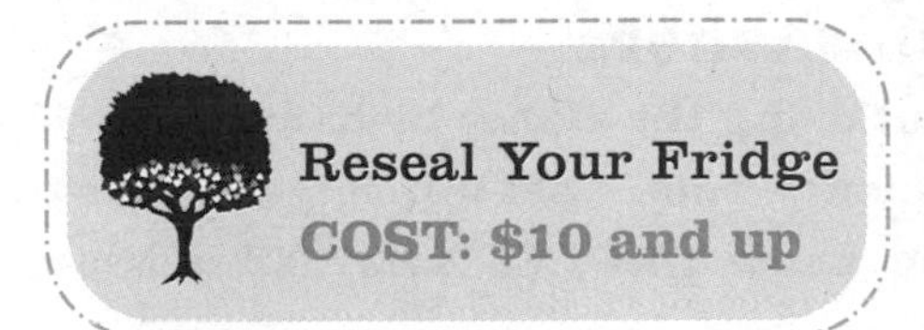

Also, make sure air can circulate around the condenser coils. If your refrigerator has coils on the back, that means leaving a space between the back of your refrigerator and the kitchen wall or cabinets.

Once or twice a year, you'll want to unplug your refrigerator and clean the coils, which are either on the back or in front, behind a kick plate. You can use a vacuum attachment or even warm, soapy water if they're greasy and grimy. Cleaning those coils enables the refrigerator to operate more efficiently.

And here's another piece of low-hanging fruit: Make sure the door seals are airtight. If you can feel cold air seeping out of your refrigerator, you're wasting a lot of energy. The good news is it's easy to install new seals, and they're readily available online or from a hardware store.

You can also adjust the thermostat inside your fridge and inside your freezer. Keep your refrigerator between 35 and 38 degrees Fahrenheit, and keep your freezer at 0 degrees Fahrenheit.

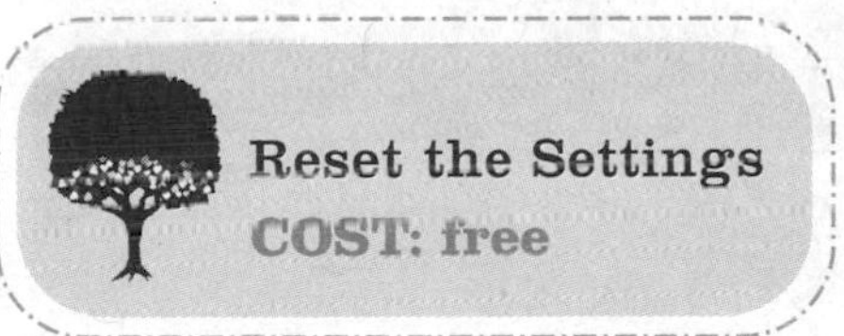

And while this may sound obvious, another easy way to save energy is to shut the refrigerator door. Some people get into the habit of leaving that door open when they're unloading groceries or trying to figure out what to cook for dinner or looking for the perfect midnight snack. This makes your refrigerator work a lot harder to keep your food cold. It's also important to avoid overcrowding your refrigerator, as restricting the airflow makes it less efficient. The freezer, on the other hand, keeps food frozen most efficiently when full.

If you do decide to upgrade your fridge, be sure to take the old one to a recycling center or call for a pickup, if that service is provided in your area. (We'll go into recycling in more detail in Chapter 3, "Recycling.")

Energy Star people, on average, refrigerators manufactured before 1993 cost over $50 more

Energy-Efficient Dishwashers

RACHELLE'S TURN

Ed used to be adamant about doing the dishes by hand. I'd just as soon use the dishwasher. I said, "Let's just get a very efficient dishwasher." You know what Ed said? "You have one. His name is Ed."

Well, guess what. It turns out using an Energy Star dishwasher is actually *more* energy efficient—and more water-wise—than washing dishes by hand. So there!

I gave Rachelle a hard time about using the dishwasher for years. The truth is, I find solace and joy and happiness in doing dishes, and I was always careful about filling up the sink with soapy water, rather than letting the water run while I was cleaning plates and pots and pans.

Still, as careful as I was, there are now Energy Star–qualified dishwashers that are even more efficient than I am.

Beyond that, a dishwasher uses hotter water than you can stand when you're hand washing. Energy Star dishwashers get that water up to 140 degrees Fahrenheit, which does a much better job of disinfecting your dishes, so it's more sanitary.

A dishwasher saves time, too—more than 230 hours a year.

Of course, you need to develop good dishwashing habits to maximize the eco-savings. First,

per year to operate than new Energy Star–qualified models. **If you use an Energy**

make sure the dishwasher is full before you run it. Using the dishwasher only saves water and energy over hand washing if you've got the dishwasher at least three-quarters full.

Also, don't use the Heated Dry feature. Instead, allow the dishes to air-dry inside the dishwasher. If you're worried about spotting, you can always use a rinse agent.

If you're like most people, you probably still rinse your dishes before you put them in the dishwasher. Rinsing dishes can waste up to 20 gallons of water per load. With most newer model dishwashers, this is no longer necessary. A grinder in the exhaust drain will cut up any residual food particles to prevent clogs, and today's detergents are designed to do all that cleaning. Even if your dishes are going to sit in the machine overnight because you don't have a full load, you're better off using the dishwasher's Rinse feature. It uses far less water than hand rinsing each plate individually.

Energy-Efficient Washing Machines

Refrigerators and dishwashers certainly aren't the only appliances that have gotten more energy efficient over time.

Full-size energy-efficient washing machines are superior to standard models on many levels. They use just 18 to 25 gallons of water per load, compared with the 40 gallons used by a non–Energy Star machine, and they extract more water from clothes during the Spin cycle, which reduces the amount of time your clothes need to spend in the dryer. This also saves wear and tear on your clothing.

Again, even if you're not ready to buy a new washing machine, you can reduce energy use—and

Star–qualified dishwasher instead of hand washing, you'll save nearly 5,000 gallons of water

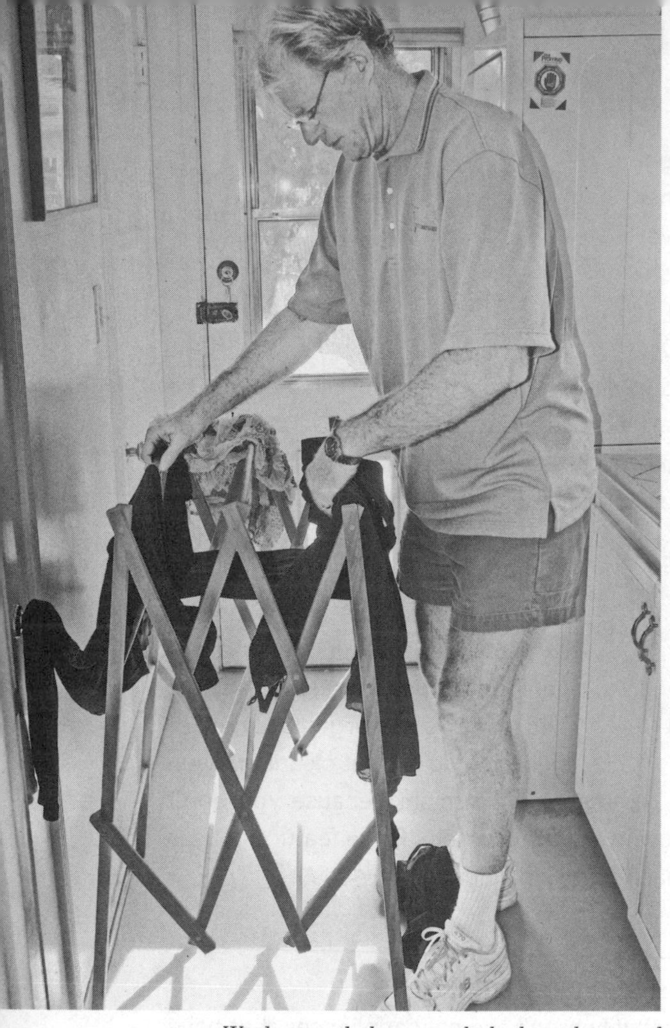

We dry our clothes on racks both outdoors and indoors—no energy required.

water use—with your current model. (When you do get a new machine, these steps will further reduce your energy use, too.) The first step is to avoid doing partial loads. Don't run the washing machine until you've got enough dirty clothes to fill it.

Also, wash your clothes in cold water. Most detergents now work very well in cold water. Even if you use warm water, you're going to be saving some energy, compared with washing clothes in hot water.

The Energy Star people haven't qualified any clothes dryers just yet, since pretty much all the dryers being sold today require the same amount of energy to operate. But there are still ways to cut down on energy use when drying your clothes. The most obvious way is not to use a machine at all. We use drying racks in our house, but you can also hang your clothes outside on a clothesline.

If you have to use a dryer, then it's best to use one that has a moisture sensor, rather than simply choosing a timed drying cycle. This way, the machine shuts off the moment your clothes are dry, rather than continuing to tumble—and

a year. Compared with a model manufactured before 1994, an Energy Star–qualified clothes

heat—your clothing. This too eliminates wear and tear on your clothes, prolonging their lives and saving on wardrobe expenses, as well as your utility bills.

Use the Dryer's Moisture Sensor
COST: free

Lastly, clean the dryer's lint filter before every load. A clogged lint filter—just like a clogged air filter for your home—will make the dryer expend extra effort and take more time to do the same amount of work.

Water Heaters

Besides washing your clothes in cold water, there are other ways to save on your water heating bill. Your water heater has a thermostat inside. That's why a hot water heater works. The natural gas comes on when the temperature drops below a certain point. I find on my hot water heater tank, I can adjust the thermostat. I have set mine to medium, on the center position, and I get water that is 110 or 115 degrees Fahrenheit.

By switching from the hottest to the medium setting, you get water that's plenty hot enough for a shower or to do dishes, and you're still saving energy. As an added safety benefit to lowering the temperature of your hot water, you remove the possibility of scalds from too-hot water in the bath or shower, or when you run water in the sink.

Another way you can save here is by putting a blanket around your water heater, if you have an older model that doesn't have thick, thick insulation like the newer heaters. A hot water heater blanket costs only $5, and many municipalities give them away for free. Check with your water provider by phone or online. A blanket keeps the hot water hotter longer, so your heater doesn't have to work so hard. (You'll find more info on water heater technology in Chapter 4, "Energy.")

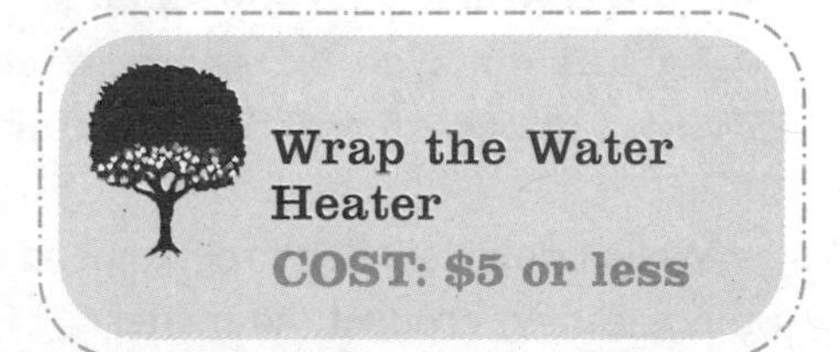

washer can save up to $110 per year on your utility bills. The efficient machine also can use

Earth-Friendly Cleaning Supplies

RACHELLE'S TURN

Most cleaning supplies are highly toxic. How many times have you gone into a bathroom that was recently cleaned and thought, "I've got to get out of here. I'm breathing toxic fumes"?

Everyone wants to protect their kids and their animals and themselves from exposure to those kinds of chemicals, so nontoxic cleaning products really make sense. Until recently, though, they just didn't work very well. I had tried them in the past and felt like they weren't good enough to satisfy me. I was always struggling with Ed over this, saying, "We need scouring powder and bleach in the house." Sometimes I bought "real" cleaning products on the sly and made my housekeepers swear not to tell.

But then, a couple years ago, a product came to us in unmarked bottles. We started using it, and—lo and behold!—it worked really well on any kind of stain, on carpets, on all kinds of surfaces. We said, "We've got to have this tested. It's got to use some kind of funky chemicals." But we had it tested, and found out it really *was* nontoxic. That cleaner became the first product we marketed under the Begley's Best name. We were so happy with it, we started a business around it.

It really is nontoxic. I use it all the time without wearing gloves, and it's never even hurt my manicure, which is really important to me. You spend some money on a manicure, and you don't want it to peel off, especially on the same day.

Ed has gone so far as to drink the stuff, which I would NOT advise. I guess Ed will do anything to make a sale!

While I definitely don't recommend that people drink my cleaner, or any other cleaning product, no matter how pure it claims to be, Begley's Best is made from environmentally responsible, natural ingredients that will not harm you, your family, *or* the environment, and you *can* drink to that!

50 percent less energy than a standard model. **There are many cleaning products made from**

Seventh Generation makes a nice laundry detergent, and Begley's Best cleaning concentrate works great as a laundry soap, too; just use a quarter cup per load. We sell it in a 64-ounce jug, so you'll get forty-eight loads out of each container.

The cleanliness of your home doesn't have to suffer from making the switch to more eco-conscious products, either. These natural cleaners dissolve grease, grime, and dirt quickly and safely. They can clean your bathroom, your kitchen, even your carpets. And you'll feel a lot better while you're using them, too. They're safer to breathe, safer for your skin, and overall they'll keep your home's air cleaner.

Insulating Your House

Another way you can really cut down on your cooling and heating bills—and save a lot of energy in the process—is by improving your home's insulation.

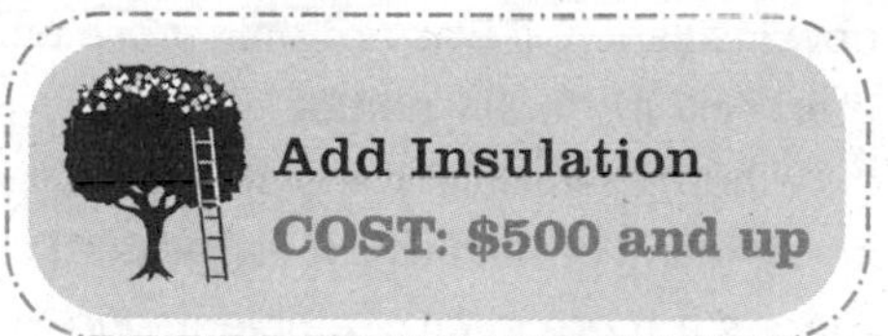

The first place you want to go is up to your attic. That's number one. Because heat rises, you lose a lot of it through the roof. In the summer, your house is also being heated by the hot sun outside, so insulation will keep it cooler and reduce cooling costs.

I had good R-30 insulation put in the attic when I moved into this house in 1988. That made the home much more energy efficient right away.

Today, experts recommend that you insulate your attic to a level of R-38, which usually means installing 12 to 15 inches of insulation, depending on the type. In especially cold climates, they recommend going as high as R-49.

One way to know if you need more insulation in your attic is to climb up there. The insulation should extend above the level of the attic floor joists—those wooden crosspieces. If you can see the joists, you probably need to add more insulation.

Looking at your insulation will provide other important information, too. If it looks dirty, then you know you have air moving through it—a sure sign of a leak that needs to be sealed *before* you install new insulation.

natural substances such as pine, cane roots, and olive seeds. **A hundred pounds of cellulose**

DIFFERENT TYPES OF INSULATION

The type of insulation you choose makes a big difference. We know more now than we did back in 1988. When I had R-30 insulation put in the attic back then, much of it was fiberglass. Then we had an earthquake here in 1994, which led to cracks and fissures in the walls and floors, and fiberglass started to migrate down into the living spaces. My friends and family had colds and allergies a lot around here. There was sneezing and runny noses. It's just not good for you to breathe that fiberglass, in part because it contains formaldehyde. It can even trigger asthma attacks.

We ultimately decided to take out the fiberglass. We had to hire people in these moon suits to do the removal. In its place we installed recycled cotton—this thick, bulky stuff that's made from old denim and from the scraps left over when companies manufacture new jeans. Once we'd installed this new insulation, it was not only more energy efficient in here, it was also quieter! And it's totally nontoxic.

Fiberglass insulation is still very common. So are rigid foam board and spray foam, both of which are essentially forms of plastic. But now you know there's a more energy-efficient *and* a more earth-friendly option. You can even install this recycled cotton insulation yourself, and you don't have to wear any special protective gear. It's that safe. While the insulation itself costs about twice as much as fiberglass, being able to install it yourself eliminates labor costs. . . .

INSULATING THE WALLS

Once you've insulated your attic, it's time to go to the next level: adding insulation to the walls of your home.

I discovered there was no insulation inside the walls of this house. Sure, they put in insulation when it was built in 1936—but they used crumpled-up newspaper! Sixty years later, there were just a few shreds left. You could read the date on a few pieces, but it was pretty far gone.

I decided to have good cellulose insulation blown into the walls to make them more energy efficient. Cellulose insulation is another popular choice for attics, too. (You also can use recycled-denim insulation inside your walls, but it must be installed when the walls are open. Denim can't be blown in after the fact like cellulose.)

insulation contains 80 to 85 pounds of recycled material. Cellulose insulation creates demand for

Ironically, the cellulose insulation used today is made from newspaper, too, but we've come a long way since 1936. Today's insulation is made from *recycled* wood fiber, primarily newsprint. This insulation is also manufactured in a way that requires far less energy than the manufacturing processes for other kinds of insulation.

Adding cellulose insulation to your walls does require the drilling of holes, so you'll have to at least touch up the exterior paint after the work gets done. Since I had a repaint scheduled for the outside of my house, I timed the installation of this new insulation to coordinate with the painter's schedule. This way, I saved money on labor, since the painting had to be done only once.

Before the painter came, I had a company go around the house and drill holes above and below the fire block in between the studs. The fire block is a small piece of wood at shoulder level, approximately, that fills the void between the vertical two-by-fours. It slows a fire from spreading because it blocks the "chimney" effect between the vertical combustible wood. Every 16 inches, on center, there are studs, which are the vertical members on any house. These guys went between the studs and blew in cellulose insulation. I think they charged me about a thousand dollars, but right away, the house got quieter, and it got more energy efficient.

DOUBLE-PANE WINDOWS

Walls and attics are not the only parts of your home that need insulation. A pretty sizable portion of your home's perimeter is made up of windows.

Windows can be one of your home's most attractive features. They provide natural light, beautiful views, and ventilation. A certain ratio of windows to floor space is even required by law—for light, for ventilation, and to provide escape routes in case of fire.

Unfortunately, most windows have a very low R-value, somewhere around R-1 or R-2. That means they can be responsible for a lot of wasted energy—up to 25 percent of your home heating bill.

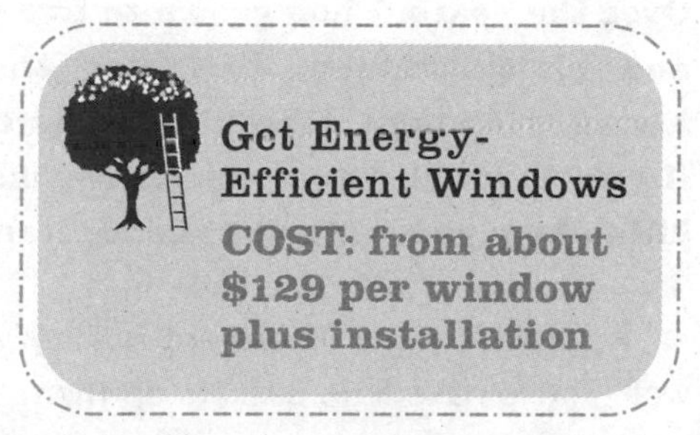

It's pretty easy to tell how efficient your windows are. Can you feel a draft when you're sitting or standing near one? Put your hand on a window. Does it feel cold in the winter or hot in the summer? If so, you're losing energy.

Double-pane windows are just what they sound like: two panes of glass (or sometimes plastic) in a single frame with a bit of air in between. That sandwich of air reduces heat transfer, keeping cold air outside from sucking the heat right out of your house in the winter. It also keeps warm air outside in the summer from transferring through a single thin pane of glass and heating up the inside of your home

RACHELLE'S TURN

I was concerned when we decided to make the switch to double-pane windows. I didn't want this adorable (albeit tiny) 1930s home to have ugly-looking windows just so Ed could save a few bucks and use less energy. Adding modern-style windows to this older house would look awful!

But Ed did his homework and actually found out that the manufacturer who had made our windows back in 1936 was still around, and they make double-pane windows that look just like our originals. There are many window companies that make double-panes in a variety of looks, so the style of your home won't be compromised.

You know, when Ed first wanted to replace all of our windows with double pane, I just thought, "Why are we spending all this money on something we already have?" I didn't really get it. But our energy usage has gone down. And what I love the most is that now I can't hear a thing! We live in a busy area, right across from a school, a block from a busy road, and a few miles from an airport. Over the years, I had grown to live with kids yelling, cars honking, and planes taking off. After the double-pane windows were installed, though, I felt like I was in the secluded countryside. Even if you're worried you won't save that much money on your energy bill (which you will), the silence itself is worth every penny.

Rachelle's right. These are quality windows. The others didn't seal as well. These have little gaskets on them. The hardware is very nice. They're

more resistant that material is, and the better it insulates. If you want to save a sizable amount

just wonderful windows, and they'll be around longer than this house will. They'll be taking them out and putting them in another house someday.

Choosing the Right Windows

Window technology has become so advanced that you can now get windows that have been fabricated specifically for your climate. Somebody who lives in Minnesota wouldn't want to install the same windows as somebody who lives in Miami. Not only is there obviously a dramatic difference in temperatures between those two regions, but there's also a difference in the amount and the strength of direct sunlight.

To meet the needs of homeowners living in different places—and working with different budgets—window manufacturers offer all kinds of options. Besides double-pane windows, there are triple- and even quadruple-pane windows. Though they are a little more expensive, triple-pane windows are a good match if you live in an environment that has harsh, long winters. It's just another added layer of protection from heat transfer.

You also can find windows with a larger airspace between panes, which also increases energy efficiency. And you can find windows with gas (usually argon) instead of air between the panes. Argon is denser and has lower conductivity than air, so it reduces heat loss—or heat gain—through the window even more.

Windows are offered with different coatings, too. Tinted glass and tinted window films are designed to reduce heat gain through windows—primarily for people in warm climates. Windows with low-e, or low-emissivity, coatings come in different styles to meet different needs. Some are designed for people in cold-weather areas to reduce heat *loss* through the windows in winter. Others are designed for people in hot climates to reduce heat *gain* through the windows in summer.

Making Any Windows More Efficient

Even if you aren't ready for the expense of replacing your windows—or if you're renting a home right now—there are ways to make the windows you already have more energy efficient.

on your heating and cooling bills, change from old single-pane windows to double-pane

RACHELLE'S TURN

Curtains, blinds, shades, and shutters are a fantastic way to add color and texture to a room. They give you a great opportunity to show off an accent color from a couch or bring a new, dramatic feel into your bedroom. They can make an impressive interior design statement. But did you know they're also a great way to save energy?

This is especially true in the winter. At night when it's cooler, just close your curtains to keep the heat in your home. In the morning when you wake up, push the curtains back and let the sun shine in to brighten and warm up your rooms. It's so simple, but it really can lower your heating bill, which saves you energy . . . and gives you more money to spend on clothes and makeup!

It's important to mention that not all window treatments go on the *inside* of your home. You can mount awnings outside—particularly on south- and west-facing windows—to block the hot summer sun.

As you know, the sun is much higher in the sky during the summer. Awnings—as well as eaves and overhangs on the outside of a house—will block that really hot summer sun, reducing your cooling costs. When the sun gets lower in the sky in the wintertime, as it moves toward the winter solstice, it's able to reach beneath the awnings and hit your windows, helping to heat your rooms for free. That is the beauty of the wraparound porches that you see on older homes, particularly in the South.

But you don't have to do a major remodel to get these same benefits in your home. Relatively inexpensive awnings are a very effective way to turn your home into a passive solar house.

You can achieve a similar effect by planting deciduous trees—trees that lose their leaves in the fall and winter. Plant them on the south side of your home—and perhaps to the west and east as well—where they will shade your house from the baking sun in summer. And in wintertime, what happens? The leaves drop off those trees, allowing the sun to warm your house.

Block the UV Rays with Window Film

COST: from $3 per square foot

windows. Curtains can physically reduce the amount of heat that escapes through your windows

In lieu of double-pane windows—or any of the more expensive window treatments—another low-cost alternative worth considering is window films. These films can be applied to any window to block a portion of the UV rays entering a room. They reduce heat gain dramatically in the summer, and they also help keep your carpet, furniture, and other possessions from fading, while you still enjoy lots of daylight.

Compact Fluorescent Lightbulbs

I *love* compact fluorescent lightbulbs. I *love* them! When I talk about pursuing the energy-saving low-hanging fruit, CFLs represent an entire orchard.

The SS *Begley* is lit completely by CFLs—*all* I have throughout the entire house are CFLs. Some of the bulbs in my house, particularly the ones in my

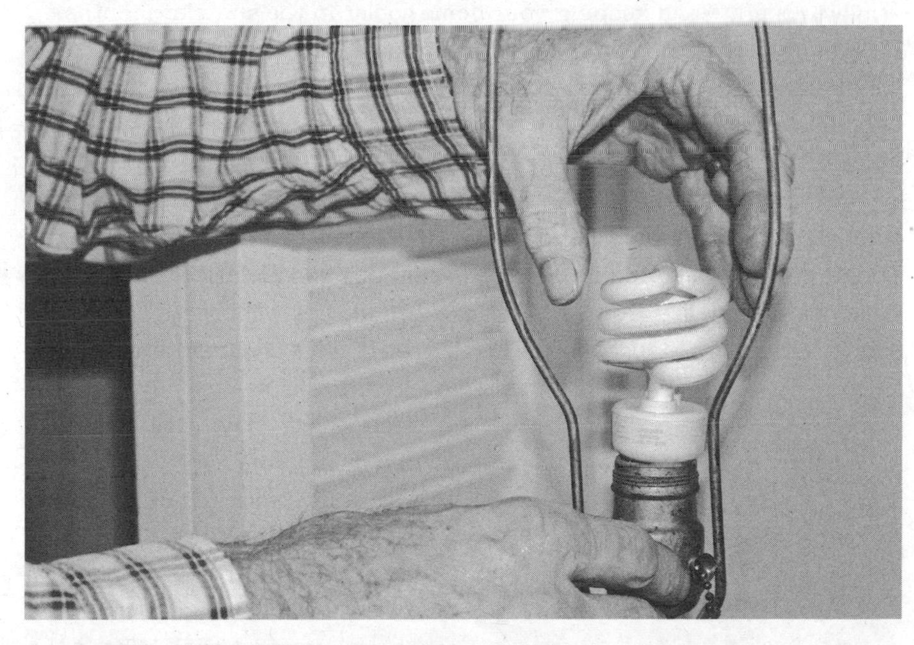

I'm such a big fan of CFLs that I would actually lobby to outlaw incandescent bulbs.

in winter and the amount of heat that comes through in summer. **The single best thing you**

home office, I bought in the early 1990s . . . and they're still burning. They save an incredible amount of energy *and* money.

The State of California and several European countries are considering passing legislation to outlaw incandescent bulbs and make the use of CFLs mandatory. People have asked me if I would support that legislation. Not only would I support it, I would lobby for it.

Here's the bottom line on compact fluorescent lightbulbs:

- CFLs use two-thirds less energy than standard incandescent lightbulbs, yet they provide the same amount of light. A CFL may draw just 18 watts of power, but it puts out 60 watts' worth of light.
- The average CFL lasts nine times longer than a normal bulb—most people say they're going to last ten years, and I've got some that have lasted as long as sixteen or seventeen years.
- Each CFL saves at least $30 in energy costs over its lifetime vs. a regular lightbulb.
- CFLs generate 70 percent less heat than regular bulbs, making them safer to operate and keeping your home cooler in the summer months.
- If every American home replaced just *one* standard lightbulb with a CFL, it would reduce greenhouse gases equivalent to the emissions of nearly 800,000 cars.

And here's great news: Even if money is really tight, you can still switch to compact fluorescent bulbs. You can get them for free from a utility like the Department of Water and Power, like Pacific Gas and Electric, like Southern California Edison, like Con Ed. A lot of these utilities will give you compact fluorescent bulbs because they've discovered that it's cheaper for them. The cheapest kilowatts they can produce these days are kilowatts saved. It's very, very difficult to site and build a new power plant—all the expense, all the red tape involved, the environmental review. And the fuel sources are natural gas and coal. What's the

can do for your home's bottom line is to change out every incandescent bulb for a CFL. If

future of that? So utility companies are really on board with saving power, not creating more and more demand from their customers.

The CFL Naysayers

Granted, there are people who look at CFLs and see problems. The mercury content, the quality of light—I've heard them all, even from my wife. These people are more comfortable with the old technology that they're used to, and they don't want to give it up. I understand that, but it's shortsighted thinking. So let me address a couple of the issues people raise surrounding compact fluorescent lightbulbs.

1. **Toxic elements in CFLs.** There's an environmental cost to everything. Look at my mountain bike. The plating processes used to create it are toxic. It has rubber tires. Energy was used both to fabricate the mountain bike and to ship it to me. But if you look at the life cycle of that bike, the amount of energy that I'm using by riding that bike around fueled by an ear of corn or a bowl of rice (human fuel, rather than fossil fuel), as opposed to what I'd use getting around in an automobile, there's no contest. I hope that everybody would agree with that.

   It's the same with a compact fluorescent lightbulb. CFLs do contain toxic elements. There's a bit of mercury in some of them, although manufacturers have been working to reduce this substantially, and some have a bit of lead in the switch, as well. But these are very small amounts, extremely small. They must be disposed of responsibly and cannot go into a landfill.

   But having said that, there's far more mercury coming out of the smokestack of a power plant that's generating electricity to power a standard incandescent lightbulb than there is in a low-energy-usage CFL. If you dispose of CFLs properly, the amount of energy that you're saving—the amount of coal that won't be burned at a power plant, of mercury that won't be going out that power plant's smokestacks—

every American home replaced just one incandescent lightbulb with a CFL, we'd save enough

over the life of that bulb, you're going to be eliminating much more mercury than you're creating. The difference is like a teaspoon to a tanker truck. Really.

2. **The quality of light is not as good.** I hear this from Rachelle a lot. And in her defense, the light from the early CFLs *was* sometimes white and harsh, much like the long tubular fluorescents used in offices and businesses. But the newer CFLs come in a wide variety of wattages with softer, warmer glows.

RACHELLE'S TURN

I remember when Ed was going to get rid of the antique chandelier in our dining room. It's from the 1930s, when the house was first built, and I loved it, but Ed decided to replace it because it wasn't "efficient." He planned to replace it with this modern thing, a real monstrosity.

I just said, "That's it. I'm outta here. I can't live here unless the chandelier stays."

So Ed put it back up and he put compact fluorescent bulbs in it. That was before the industry had come out with CFLs that could be dimmed, so your choice was either on or off, and the light was really harsh back then. It was horrifying. In the end I just left the chandelier off and lit candles in the dining room. (Fortunately I love candles.)

But compact fluorescent lightbulbs have gotten so much better, thank goodness! We've reached a point where I can even turn on the chandelier again! The light is softer, and you can dim them, too. So Ed added a dimmer switch to the chandelier and he put in the newer bulbs, and it's fine now.

I've even found a way to live with some of the older CFLs that we have that are still working—and Ed will be the first to tell you that these things last forever. I just put a lamp shade on them to change the color and soften the light. So believe me, fluorescent lighting in your home doesn't have to be horrible.

Concerns About Water

Water use—or rather water *waste*—is a hot topic in our house. Rachelle still doesn't seem to understand why I keep after her about wasting water. Well, here's why.

Many experts theorize that water is going to be our next crisis, because of global climate change. If there is less snow in mountainous regions, which most climatologists agree is going to happen, then a water shortage will come. There will be periods of rain, certainly, but right now we have a big savings account banked in all that snow. With global warming, we'll have less snow in the future, so this "cash" in the form of rain will be passing by quickly. Instead of freezing and staying in a "snow bank," it will wash right on by and we won't be able to use it fast enough.

Those same experts say there will be flooding and other problems, too, but the worst part is there will simply be a lot less water, and we won't have this wonderful reserve. Nature has been doing it this way for years: Build up a stockpile and then release it when the snow melts from the Sierras and our other water storage banks. Year in, year out, you could pretty much count on it. But that cycle has been broken, many experts feel, and if they are correct, it will be very, very dicey for places like Southern California, where nearly all of our water comes from other areas. We get it from the Owens Valley, from the California Aqueduct, from the Colorado River. And if one leg of that stool gets shaved off, we're going to teeter and eventually fall.

Water comes at such high environmental cost for the fish, and for the people, too. In the Owens Valley lots of folks have respiratory problems and what have you. A bit of a dust bowl thing has occurred there. It's been an ongoing problem for many, many years because of the way they sold off their water rights so we could thrive here in Southern California. But the plant and animal species, as well as the human population, are paying dearly for this transaction.

Water also requires a great deal of energy to move from place to place. One of the biggest energy bills for the infrastructure of the State of California is pumping water. Certainly it takes a great

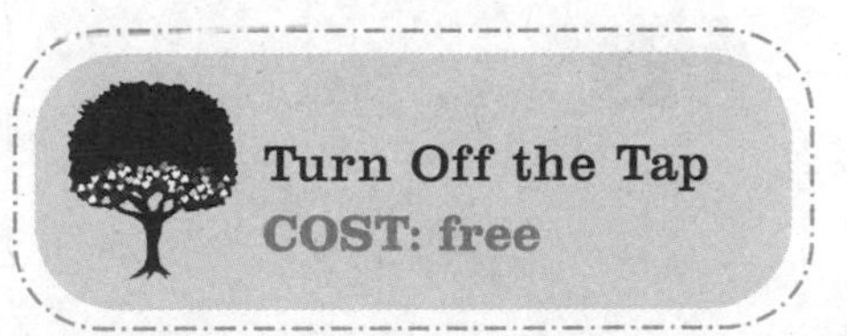

showers really do use a lot of water—between 5 and 10 gallons every minute. A leaking toilet

deal of energy to pump water into the California Aqueduct. Gravity does most of the work getting water through the William Mulholland project from the Owens Valley, I'm told, but once in the California Aqueduct, the water must be pumped over mountain ranges. The water that comes from the Colorado River also requires a tremendous amount of energy.

Ways to Save Water

How can you save water? There are so many ways. Some involve simply changing a habit. Others might involve changing a piece of equipment in your home. But none are really all that complicated, when you come right down to it.

RACHELLE'S TURN

When I first moved in with Ed, he would come in and turn off the water when I was brushing my teeth. It never occurred to me that I was wasting water. I just liked the sound of water running while I was brushing my teeth; it seemed comforting. I thought everyone did it. Well, not in this house. I've learned about a million different ways to save water, and I'm getting much better at it. I know, because Ed shows me the water bill every month!

Sometimes Rachelle will turn on the water in the bathroom and then go, "Oh, wait. I've gotta call Jennifer." And then she'll get on the phone and the water will be running and all I can see in my mind are fish flopping in the mud in Northern California.

When you're brushing your teeth—or doing anything—turn off that water if you're not actually using it. That's really important. It's an easy habit to change and it definitely saves water. Fill the sink and use that water to rinse off your razor while you're shaving, rather than leaving the water running. If you're doing just a few dishes, put the stopper in the sink and fill it partway with

can waste up to 60 gallons of water *per day.* Switching to a water-saving shower head or

soapy water, rather than letting the water run while you do the dishes or running the dishwasher with just a partial load inside.

You also can purchase a flow restrictor for the tap, not to mention a low-flow showerhead to reduce water usage.

RACHELLE'S TURN

Ed eventually started timing my showers. He'd come in and say, "You know, you've been in there for like ten, fifteen minutes!" I'm like, "How do you know?" And he was standing outside the bathroom timing me, telling me how many gallons of water I had used. I've cut back since then. Ed can tell you exactly how many gallons of water I've saved ever since!

I do a navy shower. I get wet and then I turn off the water while I soap up. And then I rinse off. I use very little shower water.

If you've ever been on shipboard when there's a long cruise and a small vessel, you're allotted a certain amount of water each day. You can drink it, you can shower with it, you can do whatever you want with it, but once you've used up your allotment, you're done, because they have only a certain amount of fresh water on board.

I try to go through every day as I if I were on board a boat, and not exceed my own personal allotment of water. Each of us has only a certain amount of fresh water. But I think there's a certain amount of denial. People waste water all the time, doing all sorts of crazy things, like hosing off their sidewalks!

I plan to teach my daughter, Hayden, about navy showers. But right now she's not using very much water, either, since she takes a bath. When we fill her bathtub, that's a fixed amount of water.

There are plenty of other ways to save water around the house, particularly in the garden. Obviously, it's smart to choose plants that don't require more water than you normally get in your area. That means avoiding tropical plants if you live in the desert. You'll also want to capture as much rainfall as you can, using a rain barrel or

installing a flow restrictor can save as much as 500 to 800 gallons of water each month. Tests some other water-collection system. That way, you can use rainwater when you need additional irrigation for your plants, instead of turning on the hose or the sprinklers. (We'll go into more detail about water-wise gardening in Chapter 5, "In the Garden and Kitchen.")

Take Care of Your Toilets

Another way to save water around your home is to replace old toilets. In 1989 I replaced every toilet in the house with a low-flush toilet. Some older toilets use as much as 6 gallons of water per flush. The new low-flow toilets use just 1.6 gallons.

In Los Angeles, city code mandates that every new toilet installed must be a low-flush model. That really makes a difference.

And here's another habit worth breaking: Don't use your toilet as a wastebasket. Why would you waste water to dispose of something that can go into an actual wastebasket or go into the compost pile or into a recycling bin?

You also can check pretty easily to see if your toilet has a leak. You just put a little food coloring or a special leak detector in the toilet tank. If that leak detector makes its way down from the tank into the toilet bowl and the water in the bowl turns that color, you know you've got a leak—and that means you're wasting water.

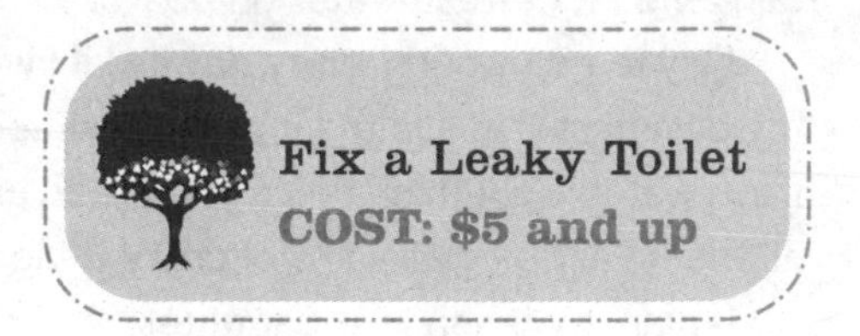

Nontoxic Paint

I've been using nontoxic paint for years, since I first moved into this house. Whenever I bought paint, I sought out the least toxic stuff available. That was a challenge in the early '90s, and even in the mid- to late '90s, it was not that easy to find earth-friendly paints.

Fortunately, it's gotten a little bit easier. There's a nice selection of stuff that won't harm the environment and that also goes on smoothly and provides good coverage. In Southern California, paints are required by law to

have shown that air inside a home can be four to eight times more polluted than air outside.

have a low level of volatile organic compounds (VOCs), but wherever you may be, you'll want to buy nontoxic paint—or nontoxic anything—whenever it's available for a project you're doing. You can even find zero-VOC paints, if you try, as well as nontoxic paint strippers.

RACHELLE'S TURN

It wasn't a challenge just to find this stuff a few years ago. It was a challenge to live with it. The nontoxic paints chipped really easily. But now they're making better and better paints, with a great choice of colors, and they're longer lasting and more durable. And that's a good thing, because my husband will never use anything else.

Using nontoxic paints *is* important. If you've gone into anyplace newly painted and smelled the intense fumes—and I kind of like the smell—that stuff's really toxic. Van Gogh and all those painters went crazy because of all the heavy metals and toxins in the paint. It's like the expression "mad as a hatter," which refers to all the chemicals used to shape the hats, which eventually caused neural damage. That toxic stuff just makes you crazy. So thank goodness they've come up with some nontoxic paints that are good for the environment and good for your health and good for your home's style, too.

Traditional paint *has* got all kinds of nasty stuff in it: petrochemicals, solvents, mercury, formaldehyde, benzene, lead, cadmium, chromium, dibutyl, and diethyl phthalate. This frightening chemical cocktail then releases VOCs into the air.

You might assume that VOCs are only a problem right after you paint, when you can actually smell that new-paint smell when you walk in a room. But it turns out paints and other finishes release low-level toxic emissions for *several years*. And it's definitely not good to be breathing this stuff.

VOCs also react with sunlight to form smog. Turn off your computer and monitor when you aren't

RACHELLE'S TURN

I love having a clean house. In fact, I'd say that I'm a neat freak. My biggest pet peeve when it comes to the house is having paint on the walls that doesn't look fresh and crisp. Walls get dingy and banged up really quickly, and I wish that we could paint them much more often than we do. These new nontoxic paints definitely make it easier for me to convince Ed that it's okay to paint the walls again. It's still a negotiation, but it's less of a battle than it used to be.

I do go into homes where I think, "Wow, the courage!" when I see the home owners' color schemes, but I've gotten a little bolder about using color now, too. At one point, my walls were all Swiss Coffee, which is a designer's fancy name for off-white. Now I'm using color as an accent, so my dining room is green, which I never would have tried before. You know, the inside of your house is an expression of your personality, so don't play it *too* safe. Just consider the colors of your furniture and the artwork before you choose a bold color. If you want to showcase your art collection, keep the walls on the neutral side.

I'm still very conservative about exterior colors. I like the basics, white and gray. Some of the stucco houses, which are common in California, can be a little bolder. But I sometimes drive through a beautiful neighborhood where I know people have paid a lot for their homes, and see that someone has painted their house bright canary yellow. So my advice is: Express yourself, sure, but try not to offend your neighbors.

Air Purifiers

Air Out Your Home
COST: free

Even if you use nontoxic paint and change your air filter regularly, the air quality inside your home could still be unhealthful.

In part, this is because a normal household is filled with chemicals (cleaners, paints, and so on), not to mention dust mites and pet dander, pollen, cooking oils, common molds (in-

using them, or simply set them to go into energy-saving, or "sleep," mode. **Home electronics**

cluding airborne bacteria), and even viruses. There's a virtual army of pollutants assailing our lungs, sinuses, and personal health in our own homes.

Also, the air inside your house might not get circulated all that well or that often. You can do wonders simply by airing out your home once in a while. Open the windows and get some cross-ventilation.

Of course, nontoxic cleaning products and nontoxic paints can reduce the number of chemicals you release into the air in your home, and you'll want to avoid things like hair spray and air fresheners.

Once you've stopped introducing toxins into the air, you're ready to take the next step and *purify* the air in your home. The purification process helps to eliminate both germs and toxic odors, improving the environment inside. I started using an electronic air purifier—a relatively small device from Advanced Pure Air that doesn't require much energy—in both my home and Rachelle's Pilates studio, which is over the garage. The air purifier has been great for improving our health and alleviating our allergies. I'll let Richard Mayer from Real Spirit USA, the company behind Advanced Pure Air, explain how the device works (see page 50).

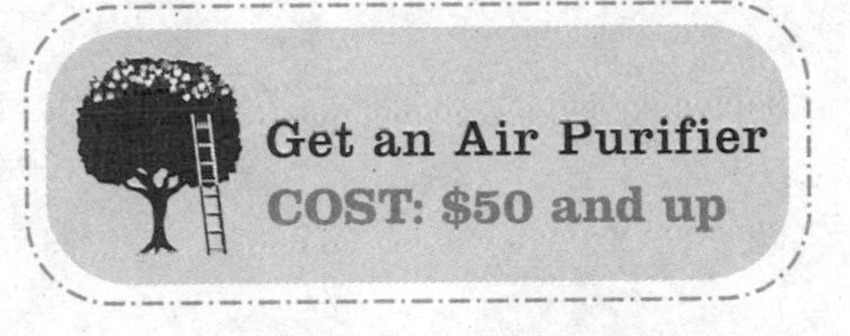

Turn Off Electronic Devices

Looking for more low-hanging fruit? You can save energy just by flipping a switch and changing some bad habits.

For instance, Rachelle doesn't understand there's this wonderful valve at the entrance to each room. It's called a light switch. Every time you flip off that switch, you save a little energy.

Rachelle will turn on a television in the living room and then she'll come into the kitchen, make dinner, and eat dinner with the television still on in the other room. You can't even hear the TV from the kitchen. So you can save a little more energy by turning off the TV when you leave the room.

items use several watts of power when they're turned off.

Ed's Green Friend: Advanced Pure Air

I started a company called Real Spirit USA to bring environmental products into people's homes to improve the quality of their lives. These Advanced Pure Air units are not just simple air filters. They are integrated, state-of-the-art air filtration and ***purification*** systems.

Instead of relying on single, limited-filtration technology, these air purifiers feature as many as nine separate air filtration and purification technologies in a single, affordable unit. These technologies include:

- **HEPA filters.** HEPA filtration, designed by NASA, is the best way to filter out solid and liquid airborne particles, including household dust, soot, pollen, and even some biological agents, like bacteria and germs. Studies indicate that HEPA filters are 99.97 percent effective at capturing harmful airborne particles as small as 0.3 microns (i.e., 300 times smaller than the width of a single human hair).
- **Activated charcoal or carbon.** This type of filter removes smells and chemicals, such as benzenes, that foul the air in homes. Activated charcoal is also very effective on smoke.
- **UV light.** UV light is highly effective in helping fight biological-based diseases caused by viruses, bacteria, and mold.
- **Photo-catalysis TiO2.** This technology enhances the UV light and helps break down the DNA of bacteria, molds, and viruses.
- **Plasma grid.** This high-voltage positive and negative charge causes the grid to attract dust, so air leaving the purifier is much cleaner than air coming in.
- **Negative ions.** These are dispersed into the air, where they attach themselves to positive particles (dust), causing them to fall to the ground, where they're picked up by the vacuum cleaner.
- **Activated oxygen.** This is extremely good at ridding the air of odors, bacteria, and mold.

By combining all of these technologies in our units, we are able to provide our customers with the healthiest, cleanest, most odor-free air possible for their homes, offices, automobiles, RVs, or even their pets' environments.

—Richard Mayer

Rachelle also regularly turns on her curling iron, then gets on the computer, then forgets about the curling iron. It turns off automatically after about 20 minutes. So then she'll turn it on again . . . and go back to the computer. She'll do two 20-minute cycles before she finally gets around to doing her hair. If I turn it off, she gets outraged—even though it gets up to full heat in 2 minutes. It doesn't get hotter at the 3-minute mark. It's as hot as it's ever going to get at 120 seconds. So all you need to do is put it on for 2 minutes—let's say a slap-happy 3 minutes—before you do your hair. Not 20 minutes, turns itself off, 20 minutes, turns itself off. There's energy to be saved there, certainly.

I'm picking on Rachelle, of course, but she's like so many people who just haven't focused on how their actions—simple little everyday actions—can make a real difference.

Fortunately, I've found some cool companies that are making it easier to save energy with no thinking required. GreenSwitch is a great example. I'll let Gregory Hood from Energy Innovation Group explain how it works.

Ed's Green Friend: GreenSwitch

The largest consumer of power in your home is your heating and air-conditioning system, which accounts for about 35 percent of the total energy used.

Household electronics items like TVs, stereos, phone chargers, and computers also draw power all the time; they're designed to stay on while they're plugged in, so you don't have to wait for them to warm up when you're ready to use them. In fact, home-electronics products like these currently consume 10 to 15 percent of the energy used in a home—and the U.S. Department of Energy predicts this number may increase to 20 percent by 2010, due to new technologies.

People who know this and want to save energy—and save money at the same time—often run around the house before they leave, turning off lights and computers and unplugging things. This can be quite a hassle, especially in a multilevel home, where people often just give up and ignore stuff on the top or lower level.

Now, there is a simple, low-cost solution for home energy management called GreenSwitch, which automates the process. With the flip of a single switch at the primary entrance/exit for your home, you can simultaneously turn off designated light switches and wall electrical outlets. Plus, GreenSwitch will set your heating and air-conditioning system to your desired temperature or turn off the system completely.

When you return home, you flip on the GreenSwitch and your wall outlets and heating/cooling system are reenergized. (You'll still have to walk through your home and turn on lights as you need them, since this allows you to continue the energy savings.)

This technology is completely wireless, so it can be retrofitted easily to any home, apartment, or condo. You can even operate it via a remote control, if you happen to use more than one entrance to your home. We also offer a split receptacle, so some things plugged into a wall outlet can remain on, while others are turned off. This is great if you have your TV and video or DVD recording device plugged into the same electrical outlet, for example; this way, the recorder can stay on while the TV gets turned off.

Another terrific use for the GreenSwitch is to "clear" your home before you go to bed, so you can save energy all night long.

A GreenSwitch should deliver a 30 to 45 percent reduction in energy use. Since the average American home uses more than 12,000 kilowatt-hours of electricity annually, a reduction in energy use of 40 percent would save 6,336 pounds of CO_2 emissions, which are created in the production of electricity.

—Gregory Hood

Home Is Where the Savings Are

So far, we've come up with dozens of ways you can save energy—and save money—in your home.

Some are really simple, like closing your curtains at night, turning off the water while you're brushing your teeth, turning off electronic devices when you aren't using them, changing the settings on your refrigerator and freezer, and waiting to run the dishwasher or the clothes washer until you've got a full load.

Others require more of an up-front expense, like upgrading to Energy Star–qualified appliances and changing to double-pane windows. But you definitely will notice the difference as soon as you make these changes. And in a few years, you'll recoup all that money you invested. Your home will be quieter, more comfortable, more energy efficient, and more environmentally sound.

But then, no matter how much you improve your home's energy use and eco-friendliness, you will eventually need to leave it. When you do, you'll need transportation—another opportunity to use, or save, energy. The next chapter looks at some of the ways you can save energy and make a difference when it comes to getting around.

TRANSPORTATION

FEET, PEDALS, AND ED POWER

2

You've got lots of choices when it comes to how you get from point A to point B.

You can drive. You can walk. You can ride a bike. You can catch a subway or a bus or a train. You can take an airplane.

How I choose to travel certainly depends on how far I have to go, and also on how soon I need to get there. But even within those confines there are choices to be made.

Ed's Transportation Hierarchy

I've given this subject a lot of thought over the years, and I've devised my own transportation hierarchy. Here it is.

1. **Walking is my first choice.** It cuts down on traffic congestion, and it's good exercise.

2. **Riding my bike is number two.** Also good exercise and great for reducing traffic. It also gives me much greater range—and gets me where I need to go faster than walking.

3. **Public transportation is next.** It not only saves money and energy, it's also like a chauffeur. I can read or do a puzzle while I'm going someplace.

4. **Next in line in the transportation hierarchy—and sorry to disappoint people who think it's my first choice—would be my electric car.** Only when I can't walk, ride the bike, or take the bus to my destination do I *then* drive my electric car. I also choose it when I have to transport heavy things or go beyond the immediate neighborhood.

5. **When I need to go beyond the range of that electric car—which has a range of about 80 to 130 miles per charge—I take a hybrid car.** If I have to get up to Santa Barbara or San Francisco, or even if I need to drive to Pittsburgh or North Carolina, I'll take the hybrid. I just drove up to San Francisco—about 250 miles—and it cost just $23 in gas each way!

6. **Finally, if I have to be in L.A. on Monday and in New York on Tuesday, I will be a good boy, shut up, and get on an airplane.** Yes, I'm burning kerosene up at 31,000 feet, and yes, I accept all the pollution associated with that for that seat on a commercial airliner. But I don't do it often, *and* I will also take steps to mitigate that pollution with a carbon offset program.

Health experts say walking 30 minutes a day will add 1.3 years to your life. Walking greatly

Walking and Hiking

So you now know my preferred form of transportation is not my electric car, not Rachelle's hybrid, not my bike. I just like to walk.

I'm fortunate to live in a neighborhood where walking *can* be my first choice. Most people say you can't walk in L.A., but there are many neighborhoods, like mine in Studio City, where you can live and work and recreate all within easy walking distance from your home.

I specifically chose this neighborhood—and found this house desirable—because of its location. I can walk to the post office. I can walk to the drugstore. I can walk to seven really good restaurants. I can walk to the supermarket. There are these great places nearby that I can walk to. And when I say walk, we're talking fractions of a mile to get major shopping done. It's good, obviously, to get exercise at my age—or any age—and you're also cutting down on pollution in the best way possible. There is very little pollution involved in walking, although you've got to factor in the life of your shoes, and the pollution involved in making them and in transporting them to you. Still, compared with any other form of transportation, it's minuscule.

So walking is always my first choice of transportation if I need to go someplace within a mile.

As for the health benefits of walking, they've been well documented.

Studies have shown that walking is good for your mind and spirit:

- It reduces your stress level.
- It improves your mood.
- It makes you mentally sharper and more alert.
- Walking releases your brain's natural "happy drugs," called endorphins.
- Regular exercise in the form of walking has even been effective in the treatment of depression.

And if walking is good for your spirit, hiking is great. Rachelle and I both like to hike. I really enjoy the quiet time, the fresh air, the beautiful views. Hiking is a wonderful way to explore nature and appreciate the beauty of

reduces the risk of diabetes, heart disease, and even cancer and glaucoma. Walking can

your environment, whether you hike up a mountain path, along a river, or through the woods.

RACHELLE'S TURN

Yeah, and Ed's really fun to hike with, too. He hikes like it's some kind of army training-camp drill. He's totally oblivious, just marching up some steep hill, and I'll be left behind. It's like, "Nice hikin' with ya." Oh, and he says fun stuff too, like "Downhill is double time."

It's not like I'm out of shape. I'm a Pilates instructor. I'm in great cardiovascular condition. But Ed really likes to take things to the extreme.

I also like to leave the trail in better condition than I found it. It goes without saying that you should never leave any trash behind, but Rachelle and I take it to the next level and pick up any trash we find along the way.

Riding a Bike

After walking, if my destination is more than a mile from home but not so far away that I need to take the car, I'll ride my bike. It's very nearly as pollution free as walking.

I ride for fitness and just for pleasure. My daughter, Hayden, and I go for bike rides all the time, and Rachelle sometimes joins us.

I also like to ride my bike for errands—for the economy, in every way. It's very inexpensive. You don't have to buy an insurance policy to ride your bike or gas to run it. You don't have to spend a lot of money to buy a bicycle, either. And bikes don't wear out. With minimal maintenance, you can keep one in good working condition for decades. I have a nice bike from the '80s that I still use, and my neighbor Bill Nye, the Science Guy, still rides a bike from 1975!

Ride Your Bike
COST: from about $50 to $100 for a basic, adult-size bike

Also, you can move really quickly around the city on a bicycle—in many cases, more quickly

lower your body fat, your cholesterol levels, and your blood pressure. **If you ride 4 miles on**

Biking is great exercise, and I love being able to pedal right past stopped traffic.

than you can in your car. When there's traffic, you just pedal right past those stopped vehicles. If you bike to work, you can vary your route, often more easily than you can commuting in a car. And with biking there's no problem with parking. Of course, it's good for the city too, because you're putting one less vehicle into traffic lanes.

So biking is good for all of us environmentally. But biking is also good for *you.* It's good for your health and has all the same benefits as walking—it's a low-impact form of exercise that reduces stress and is good for your mind and spirit. I can go much farther on a bike than I can on foot. I've biked 80 miles in a day. I don't have the time anymore to do those long bike rides, but I will bike somewhere that is 15 miles away, and biking over the hill into Hollywood or Beverly Hills is no big deal to me. It's not like, "Ooh, I can't do it. Am I going to be okay?" It's no problem. I don't think twice about making a 30-mile round-trip bike ride.

a bike instead of driving, you will keep 15 pounds of pollutants out of the air we breathe.

RACHELLE'S TURN

For many years, people would say, "There goes Ed, riding his bike to the *Vanity Fair* party." And I would be thinking, "I can't believe he rode his bike here." But then all the paparazzi would be all over him, and I would think, "Well, that's pretty cool." People thought he was a bit nuts, and they didn't take him seriously. And that was sorta hard.

Now, being green is so cool! You've gotta get a gimmick if you're gonna get ahead in Hollywood, and a lot of people seem to be choosing the green gimmick. Only with Ed, it's no gimmick. He's been doing it for years. And no one is laughing now!

One reason I love bicycles so much is because they're the most energy-efficient machines for ground transport that man has ever invented. Maybe you could say a sailboat is more energy efficient, since you can use the wind to take you around the globe. But as far as ground transportation, there's nothing better than a bike. You can literally go 30 miles being fueled only by a bowl of rice or a cup of beans. I'd say that's pretty good mileage.

If you need to go longer distances, there's another option now: a hybrid bicycle. Unlike a hybrid car, which runs partly on an electric engine and partly on a gasoline internal-combustion engine, a hybrid bike runs partly on an electric engine and partly on human energy. Rachelle got me an iZip hybrid electric bike for my birthday in 2006, and I love it. I'll let Larry Pizzi from Currie Technologies, which makes the iZip, explain more.

Ed's Green Friend: iZip

Electric bicycles come in many shapes, sizes, and capabilities, but they all share the ability to power the bike solely by human power—pedaling—or with electric power, either to supplement the rider or as the sole motive energy. This category of bike is also called *pedalec*, a term used primarily in European countries to classify pedal-assist vehicles.

Here's how it works. Stored energy, in the form of a battery, feeds an electric motor, which then propels the unit. Endurance, speed, and distance are limited by the amount of energy stored and by the rate of discharge to the motor.

Great strides in improving performance have been made in recent years, thanks to innovative technologies that have created batteries with higher energy densities that charge faster and weigh less. The best systems may incorporate sophisticated battery management computer chips that both protect the battery and enhance performance. The digital revolution also has had a major impact through the creation of microprocessors that efficiently calculate and send precise bursts of energy to the motor.

Another major innovation has been the creation of a link between human and motor-driven power. The result is a form of hybrid power whereby pedaling force triggers a proportional energy contribution to the motor. This linkage significantly increases range and, depending on how an electric bike is tuned, it can raise top speed substantially without too much deterioration to that range.

With microprocessors doing much of the work behind the scenes, throttles and other annoyances can be disposed of, creating a simple interface and a more bike-like experience.

Electric bikes are an efficient alternative for urban transportation, for commuting shorter distances, and now even for fitness and fun, as on the hybrid pedalec versions that allow a rider to travel greater distances at a faster pace.

Compared with automobiles, the hybrid bike's energy use and carbon footprint are infinitesimal. So, in the process of enjoyment and practical use, you can really benefit the planet, plus get some light exercise for your own well-being. And, of course, operating costs are far lower than for most other means of transportation.

Ed now has several iZip bikes, and they free him from his dependence on the automobile for daily situations, such as shopping, buying a paper or coffee, visiting friends, and generally getting around. In the process, he enjoys a better standard of living with a closer connection to the world, and to his own emotional and psychic center, while helping maintain his own physical vibrancy.

—Larry Pizzi

Public Transportation

When walking or biking simply isn't practical, I always look to public transportation before hitting the garage door opener. By public transportation, of course I mean buses, trolleys, subways, commuter trains, and light-rail service—even cable cars, if I'm in San Francisco. The official definition of public transportation, according to the American Public Transportation Association (APTA), also includes paratransit services for senior citizens and people with disabilities, as well as ferries and vanpool services.

You could say public transportation is like carpooling, on a grander scale. Carpooling clearly reduces the use of fossil fuel: It reduces tailpipe emissions, it saves money, and it reduces traffic congestion. Using public transportation obviously takes carpooling to a whole other level, with dozens—if not hundreds—of people able to share a ride at the same time.

For public transportation to make sense for you as a regular option, of course you need to live in a place that makes it convenient. Luckily, I do. A natural gas bus stops at a corner near my home, and I can take it—only one stop—to a big, beautiful electric subway that goes to many parts of Los Angeles and connects to other light-rail systems that go to other parts of the city. So I'm very fortunate on one hand, and very clever on the other hand, to have chosen this home, where it's easy for me to get to the places I want to go by walking, biking, and taking public transportation.

If I have to go downtown or into Hollywood, I often take the subway. I can avoid the traffic, and if I buy tokens, it costs me just $1.10 per trip. You can't even park downtown for $1.10!

And when I'm on the subway, I can leave the driving to someone else. I can do a Sudoku puzzle or a crossword puzzle or the Jumble. Occasionally, I have to go downtown to testify for some City Council meeting or the L.A. Board of Supervisors. In that case, I can review the material I'm going to talk about on the way down there, or I can read the newspaper and relax. The same on the way back. It's very convenient.

Ride a Bus or a Train
COST: around a buck and up

And let me be clear that I take public transportation by choice. There are many people who are

If just one person in your family uses public transportation regularly—as a way to get to work

dependent on it for financial reasons. But though I have alternatives, I take public transportation pretty regularly—just not with my wife.

RACHELLE'S TURN

I did take public transportation with Ed one time when we were first dating. We were going out to some restaurant. I was in high heels, which I usually don't wear, and a miniskirt. We got on the bus at West Hollywood, and the bus didn't come directly over to the Valley, so we had to change buses—on Western Avenue, underneath a strip club, next to the freeway. At midnight! I was like, "I can't believe this. I'm not doing this! I'm not doing this! I'm not this dedicated." We got home, finally, but, clearly, our transportation choices were a major source of conflict.

Today, we've reached a compromise. Mostly, I drive my hybrid. And, yes, I have come to understand the benefits of public transportation. I even use the carpooling analogy sometimes when I'm talking to friends—you know, explaining about Ed.

And if you want to know the truth, I don't mind riding the subway. It reminds me of New York City, only cleaner and newer. But I still let Ed ride the bus on his own.

THE BENEFITS OF PUBLIC TRANSPORTATION

Rachelle's opinion of buses notwithstanding, we do have a pretty good transportation system in L.A., given the size of the city and the number of people who are transported. This city is so spread out, from Trancas to Santa Clarita to Pomona to the Orange County line. That's a lot of territory and a lot of people. There's no transit system anywhere else on the globe that takes more people over greater distances every day.

For my money, transportation systems need to be multifaceted. They need to have many different tools in the toolbox. The backbone of the transportation system, the spine of it, here in L.A.—and in most cities—is the bus system. Even in New York City, which is famous for a tremendous subway network, the bus system still carries almost half as many riders as the subway. That's a significant number. And in a city like L.A., the bus system carries nineteen times as many passengers as the light-rail system.

or school or wherever he or she needs to go—your household can save more than $1,400

So the city's transportation system is like a big-city hospital. Most of the work is done with sutures and tongue depressors and thermometers, the basic tools. The bus system is part of that basic infrastructure.

But you still need a big MRI unit, too! And that's the subway or the light-rail system. It's another important tool in the transportation toolbox. We still need to get people off the roads entirely, not just create more bus lanes.

According to the APTA, throughout the United States as a whole:

- There are more than 6,400 providers of public and community transportation.
- From 1995 through 2006, public transportation ridership increased 30 percent, while the U.S. population increased only 12 percent. During the same period, use of U.S. highways increased only 24 percent—less than the growth rate for public transportation. That's good news.
- In 2006, Americans took 10.1 *billion* trips on public transportation, the highest ridership level in forty-nine years.

Using public transportation is certainly a good way to save money, too.

Augmenting your driving with public transportation could even eliminate your family's need for an additional car, and that's a way to save *real* money.

Public transportation is also a great way to save fuel. According to the APTA:

- Public transportation use in the United States saves 1.4 billion gallons of gasoline each year, or nearly 4 million gallons of gasoline per day.
- That eliminates the need for thirty-four supertankers of oil to make their way to the United States each year.
- It also eliminates 140,769 local fuel deliveries, those big tanker trucks that clog our streets on their way to local gas stations, not to mention the wear and tear they exact on our roads.

Public transportation also reduces traffic congestion, which reduces travel time for everyone on the road. In 2003, according to the APTA, public transportation in America's most congested cities saved travelers 1.1 billion hours in travel time.

worth of gas in a single year. Public transportation usage saves the equivalent of 300,000

All that public transportation use reduces emissions dramatically. When you compare its per-passenger mile against private vehicles, public transportation produces 95 percent less carbon monoxide (CO), 90 percent less volatile organic compounds (VOCs), and about half as much carbon dioxide (CO_2) and oxides of nitrogen (NOx). Those savings really add up.

Electric Cars

There are times when I just need more flexibility than public transportation can offer, and on those occasions, I turn to my electric car. Some places are hard to reach via bus, light rail, or subway, and of course, I'm at the mercy of their schedules. Driving the electric car is also much more convenient when I need to transport a lot of stuff or heavy items.

Let me be clear here: By *electric car,* I mean a vehicle powered *exclusively* by an onboard battery pack. That's different from a hybrid vehicle, which has both an electric motor *and* a gasoline-powered internal-combustion engine. When I say *electric car,* I mean 100 percent electric.

And here's one of my favorite things about the electric car. As I've mentioned, I have solar panels on the roof of my house. The rooftop is a perfect place to gather energy, and that energy then gets stored in a battery system in my garage.

Drive an Electric Car
COST: from about $6,800 for a low-speed "neighborhood" vehicle

If you charge your electric car using any kind of green power—by using solar panels like I have on my roof, or by buying green power from your utility company (more on that in Chapter 4, "Energy")—then your electric car can be a true, 100 percent zero-emissions vehicle.

Now technically, by definition, a zero-emissions vehicle creates zero pollution while it's *in use.* (As in all things, there's still pollution created in building the vehicle and in transporting it to the dealership, and so on.) But a zero-emissions vehicle, or ZEV, creates zero pollution while you own and drive it because it produces

automobile fill-ups *every single day.* You can't make gasoline on the roof of your house, but

- zero tailpipe emissions
- zero evaporative emissions (gasoline can escape from various parts of an internal-combustion-engine vehicle's fuel system and evaporate into the atmosphere)
- zero emissions as the result of the gasoline refining process
- zero emissions as the result of the transport and sale of gasoline

Plus, an electric car doesn't even have—or need—an onboard emissions-control system, which can go bad over time and allow further polluting emissions into the atmosphere.

So when we're talking about green cars, an electric car is the greenest of the green. That's why I'm a longtime believer in this technology. I bought my first electric car in 1970. Of course, electric cars have come a long way since then.

RACHELLE'S TURN

You know how dependent we are on our cars, especially in L.A.? Well, when Ed and I started dating, he would not *get into* a gasoline-powered vehicle, or only in the most dire of circumstances.

He did have an electric vehicle, but back then electric vehicles were not as reliable as they are today—and that's putting it mildly! I remember going out and then running out of electricity many times. One time, we were going down the hill on Laurel Canyon and the car caught fire!

And then there was the time when I was in labor with our daughter, Hayden. Ed wanted to drive me to the hospital in his electric car; I said, "Oh no, we are *not* taking an electric car today." It probably would have made it fine, but just the thought of running out of electricity with me in labor—no way was I going to take that risk.

Today, things are really different. Now, when we go out we always take Ed's car. This electric car is great. I love it, especially now that gas is over $3 a gallon, 'cause we have solar power, so it's like we're not really paying to fuel the car.

I charge my Phoenix Motorcars sport utility truck using my home's solar power.

AREN'T YOU JUST MOVING THE POLLUTION TO THE POWER PLANT?

Of course, not everyone has a solar power system that can charge their electric car. Most people purchase their electricity from their utility company.

Naysayers will tell you that electric cars just shift the pollution from a car's tailpipe to an electricity-generating power plant's smokestack, but here again I think the upside far outweighs any downside, and I'll explain why. There are three reasons you're not just moving the same pollution to the power plant:

1. YOU'RE MAKING USE OF OFF-PEAK CHARGING, WHICH IS HIGHLY EFFICIENT AND WHICH CREATES NO NEW POLLUTION. When you're charging an electric car, you're making use of an incredible inefficiency that none of the naysayers talk about. Anybody who knows anything about power generation—talk to the people who run Southern California Edison, the Department of Water and Power, Duke

***and* it can power your car.** Imagine getting free gasoline for the rest of your life. That's what

Power—will tell you the same thing. All big power plants have excess capacity during off-peak hours that is not being utilized. We're not talking about a little Honda generator that is shut down at night when there's less demand. These big power plants run all night—they have to, just given the nature of the way they were constructed, the way they're maintained, and the way they work. At some power plants, *some* of the generators can be shut down, but most keep them *all* running all night.

To deal with this excess capacity, utility companies build *shedding facilities.* They get rid of the extra power that's generated at night—since most power plants keep producing power at the same rate 24/7, and since peak usage for electricity occurs in the middle of the day.

So a shedding facility uses up all that extra power at night. In the L.A. area, a shedding facility actually pumps water uphill at night from Lake Castaic to Lake Hughes. They pump water uphill at night! Did you know that? They pump it uphill at night, and then they run it downhill during the day when they need power.

Why do they do this? Because they have these big generators that are running all night that produce *wasted* electrons. Were they liquid, someone would be literally pouring these wasted electrons down a storm drain.

Utility companies are making lots of electricity that's wasted. That's why they're always asking their customers, "Can you do your laundry at night? Can you vacuum later in the day?" In general, you should try to time as much of your electricity use as you can for off-peak hours. Some appliances can be set to go on later, like your breadmaker. Using power off-peak means you are using power that would otherwise be wasted rather than making the power company make more, and that's very efficient.

And this is why there's less pollution from an electric car, even if you're not charging it on solar. You're making use of these free electrons, not adding to the energy drain on the power grid during peak hours. Unless you work at an all-night doughnut shop or a twenty-four-hour pharmacy, you're probably going to be driving during the day and you'll recharge your car's battery at night. You may do a little bit of charging during the day, but by and large you're going to come home and plug in the electric car; that's off-peak. You're not causing the utility company to produce more electricity, you're using what they're already producing that goes unused.

it's like when you charge your electric car with your own solar energy. While there is a cost to

Now, keep in mind, when we hit a million electric vehicles on the road, that will be a different story. Then we'll need to get some new solar, wind, geothermal, or other kind of green energy going into the grid to keep all these electric cars charged. But for now, there's a lot of perfectly good energy going to waste out there. In fact, enough to power up to a million new electric cars—if they were spread out evenly across the country—without creating any new pollution.

2. IT'S MUCH EASIER TO CONTROL POLLUTION AT ONE POWER PLANT THAN IT IS IN A MILLION TAILPIPES. People monkey around with the emission controls on their cars. They give the guy at the smog-check station some bills and say, "I need to pass this test." You can't do that at a power plant. I mean, there are power plants that have tried to do that—to cheat—but they're in violation and are going to court. It's much harder to control a million tailpipes than it is one smokestack.

3. AND ALSO—I SAVED THE BEST FOR LAST—25 PERCENT OF THE GASOLINE CONSUMED BY EVERY CAR OUT THERE IS USED WHEN IT'S NOT EVEN IN MOTION! It's called idling, and it uses up 25 percent of the gasoline you pump into the tank.

Here's why. You're usually not driving across the plains of Nebraska. If you live in a city like L.A., there's constant stop-and-go traffic. You sit at the stoplight or the stop sign, waiting for people to cross the street. All the while, your car needs gas to keep it humming—even though you're not going anywhere.

With a hybrid or electric car, the minute you take your foot off the accelerator, you're using zero amps. Zippo. You may have your air conditioner on or your CD player or your lights, but these use very little power. The big demand on the car—the motor—is using no power when you're stopped, and that's a *big* efficiency.

Convinced?

AN ELECTRIC CAR'S RANGE

Now, I can't go everywhere with my electric car, for the simple reason that it can only go so far on a single charge. The range of my last electric car, a

install the solar panels and for the battery system, once it's in, you essentially get all that

Toyota RAV4 EV, was 80 miles under average driving conditions. And that was round-trip—unless I had plenty of time and a charger on the other end (because it can take up to 8 hours to charge an electric vehicle's battery from empty to full).

Practically, I could only go 40 miles each way in that car. That was enough to get me to most places I would normally drive. For example, it's a 17-mile drive to Los Angeles International Airport. The other end of the Valley, Chatsworth, is also about 17 miles away. Hollywood is just 7 miles away. Downtown is 13 miles away. Acton, where I often had to go for film shoots, was 38 miles each way. I could make it there and back, but I couldn't go any farther. If there was roadwork and I had to make a detour, I'd end up charging somewhere.

So yes, an electric vehicle's finite range is somewhat of a limitation, but it has increased dramatically since my very first electric car, which could go only 15 miles between charges. And battery technology continues to improve. Today, many companies are focused on increasing the amount of energy that can be stored in ever smaller, ever more durable batteries—even batteries that use greener materials. On the one hand, it's part of an ongoing trend toward miniaturization—things like computers and radios and calculators and cell phones getting ever smaller. And it's also part of an ongoing trend toward better, smarter batteries that can hold more energy and that don't need to be fully charged—and fully discharged—each time you use them. You've seen improvements like these in your cell phone batteries, digital camera batteries, and laptop computer batteries. Those advances in battery technology mean electric vehicles' range will no doubt get even better in coming years.

RACHELLE'S TURN

So what's it like to drive an electric car? You turn it on and you hear nothing. It's a go-kart. It's very quiet. You get accustomed to the sound of a gasoline engine, so when you turn on the electric car and it just goes *click,* you wonder, "Is it on?" Many times, when we've left the car with the valet, they go *click, click, click,* and try to make that *vroom* sound. When we get our car back they say, "It's broken!" You have to be extravigilant about pedestrians because they can't hear you

energy for free! **According to the Bureau of Transportation Statistics, the average American**

coming—there's no indicator—no beep, beep, beep. That's the danger of it. But it goes fast. I like it. It's fun.

And I'm all for Ed's new electric car. It's great. The only downside is how far you can go on a charge.

A QUICK HISTORY

Some people think electric vehicles are a new idea, but they've been around for centuries. A Scotsman named Robert Anderson invented the first crude electric carriage powered by a nonrechargeable type of battery between 1832 and 1839. Thomas Davenport is credited with building the first practical electric vehicle—not a horseless carriage, but a locomotive—in 1835. Jump ahead to 1891, and William Morrison of Des Moines, Iowa, built the first successful electric car in the United States.

Recently, I got to ride in a 1909 Baker electric car owned by Jay Leno. What an amazing vehicle. It was way ahead of its time. Back in 1909, cars didn't even have electric starters. They had gas headlamps. But this car was *fully* electric. Interestingly, it was designed for women, for them to go shopping, since it was clean and quiet and quite elegant inside, with a vase for fresh flowers and a mirror mounted on the door to check their makeup. It's incredible just how advanced this car was.

Sadly, by the 1920s, electric cars had lost their allure. Cheap and plentiful gasoline—and the longer range of cars with internal-combustion engines—temporarily made electric cars all but unsalable.

Then we had that first gas crisis in the early 1970s—and, about the same time, people became concerned about pollution—and all of a sudden, there's an interest in alternative fuels again. The government got involved, too, and began pushing the companies that manufacture automobiles to make vehicles that would get better gas mileage and create less pollution. In 1976 Congress passed the Electric and Hybrid Vehicle Research, Development, and Demonstration Act. Its goal was to encourage development of new technologies, like improved batteries, electric motors, and other hybrid-electric components.

Electric vehicle development really got a boost in 1990, when the California Air Resources Board (CARB) passed the Zero-Emission Vehicle Mandate. It required 2 percent of the vehicles in California to have zero emis-

drives 29 miles per day—well within the range of an electric vehicle. **Some people actually**

sions by 1998, and 10 percent by 2003. Unfortunately, CARB was not able to enforce its policy. In 2002 General Motors and Chrysler—along with the Bush administration—sued CARB to repeal the mandate. By 2003 CARB had weakened the mandate to the point that automakers could get zero-emission vehicle credits for non-ZEV vehicles.

Now there's almost no *incentive* for automakers to develop electric vehicles, which is why GM, Toyota, Ford, Honda—companies that offered electric cars just a few years ago—have all gotten out of the electric car business. They've got some interesting pure-electric concept cars, but not one of these companies offers a pure-electric vehicle that you can buy today.

So what are your choices, if you want to drive an electric car? Several smaller companies have been developing electric vehicles on their own. After doing a lot of research, I've gotten involved with a company called Phoenix Motorcars. I now drive the company's sport utility truck (SUT), and I'm a big fan. It's a five-passenger vehicle, and its new battery technology has increased my range to more than 100 miles per charge. I'll let my friend Dan Elliott, the company's CEO, tell you more about it.

Ed's Green Friend: Phoenix Motorcars

Electric vehicles are giving drivers across America hope that their days of dealing with soaring gas prices are coming to a close. Many consumers question electric vehicles, simply because they aren't informed as to what exactly a battery-run vehicle is and how it can positively affect their lives.

Electric vehicles (EVs) produce no exhaust fumes and, if they're charged using most forms of renewable energy, minimal pollution. Many are capable of acceleration that is equivalent to—or, in some cases, exceeds that of—conventional gasoline-powered vehicles.

Simply put, EVs reduce dependence on petroleum. They help to reduce global warming by alleviating the greenhouse effect. They are significantly quieter than internal-combustion vehicles, and they do not produce noxious fumes.

So how does an all-electric vehicle work? Electric vehicles are powered by an electric motor that uses rechargeable batteries rather than a gasoline engine. Electric motors have the ability to convert energy back into electricity through ***regenerative braking,*** so when the driver of an electric vehicle steps on the brake pedal, it can actually recharge the car's batteries. Regenerative braking can be used to reduce the total energy requirement of a trip, as well as reduce the wear on the vehicle's brake system.

Since Ed purchased his first electric vehicle more than thirty years ago, he has experienced firsthand the progression of battery technology—and that progression has been dramatic. Our vehicles are powered by UQM Technologies' propulsion system, using Boshart Engineering's certification process, and they are equipped with a nontoxic, revolutionary Altairnano Nanosafe battery pack. These three factors make it possible for Phoenix Motorcars' all-electric, zero-emission vehicles to reach speeds of more than 95 mph with a range of 100-plus miles per charge. They also produce a serious 480 lb-ft of torque—as much torque as the 500-horsepower internal-combustion engine that powers the new Ford Shelby GT500 muscle car! Our vehicles also have a battery pack life of more than 12 years.

Phoenix Motorcars are not only all-electric and environmentally friendly, they also have the creature comforts people have come to expect in a vehicle that they drive every day—things like air-conditioning and heat, power windows, and power door locks.

In the last two years, the worldwide media coverage of global warming and the high cost of our dependence on fossil fuels has intensified. For those of us in the electric-powered transportation industry, it would be easy to say, "It's about time." But that viewpoint is too simple. It is, however, the right time for meaningful action. As a matter of fact, Phoenix Motorcars is poised to meet the growing demand of consumers who want a cleaner, more responsible alternative to gasoline-powered vehicles, and we consider our company an early leader in the mass production of full-function, zero-emission, green electric trucks and SUVs.

As Ed has said, "With a car like this Phoenix Motorcars SUT, you don't have to compromise on performance or space—you get it all!" And if you do like Ed does and plug it into your solar power system at home to charge, you literally create a ***zero*** carbon footprint!

—Dan Elliott

INFRASTRUCTURE ISSUES

So, given their many advantages, why doesn't everyone own an electric vehicle? Well, for one thing, municipalities are making it harder, not easier, to operate one. In the mid-'90s, California instituted special parking spots where EV owners could recharge their cars midtrip. Today, these have almost vanished. Why? To understand this, you need to know a bit about battery technology. Until recently, when you bought an electric car, you also got a charging station, which most people mounted in their garage. I had the charging station for my Toyota RAV4 EV mounted in my garage, and I charged it at home almost exclusively. It was rare that I could do my charging elsewhere—very rare. That was partly because my life had become very busy, but it also was because L.A. had become less friendly for electric vehicles. Precious few of those electric vehicle charging stations were still in existence by 2007.

That's because the major car companies—GM, Toyota, Honda, Chrysler—that were making electric cars during the '90s and right up until recently didn't come to a consensus in terms of what type of charging system to use. Instead, they came up with two—well, really three—different charging disciplines. Think of it as VHS vs. Betamax vs. DVDs. Some of their electric cars used large-paddle chargers—these big flat plastic pieces that had to be plugged into the right-size hole in the right type of charging station. Other companies used small-paddle chargers. Both of these setups used what's called an inductive charging system. The third type of charging system was a conductive style.

None of these formats were interchangeable at all, so you could only use a charging station designed specifically for your vehicle's system. This made it really hard for people to charge their electric cars anywhere but at home, and it upset people who didn't own electric cars. They'd see a parking space reserved for electric vehicles—with a charging station—and they'd wonder, "Why don't I see any electric vehicles charging there?"

The good news is that most *new* electric cars—including my new Phoenix Motorcars SUT—have the charger built right in. You no longer *need* a separate charging station at home or anywhere else. You plug your car into a standard 220-volt electrical outlet, just like the one for your clothes dryer at home. Because these cars are designed to charge on 220 current, they

consider 1900 to be the heyday of the electric car. At the time, 28 percent of the roughly 4,200

charge a lot faster than older models. It takes just four or five hours to fully charge the battery pack.

In a pinch, you also can plug into a standard 120-volt outlet, the standard wall outlets you have in your home. That makes charging on the road easy, if you find yourself running low on range. Instead of having to look for a special charging station, you look for any 120-volt outlet. You can find them in parking garages. You can find them at restaurants. Those 120-volt outlets are in a lot of places.

True, it will take about twice as long to charge on 120-volt power as it will on 220-volt power, but it's nice to have that option. It just makes these new electric cars even easier to live with.

Rachelle's Hybrid

RACHELLE'S TURN

Today's electric cars are great, but I wasn't willing to be limited by the range of an electric car. In 2001, when I was ready to get a new car, I decided I wanted a Volvo because of its safety features, until Ed made me this deal: "If you get a Volvo, you pay for it. And if you get this newfangled Toyota hybrid thing, even though we don't know how well it works, I'll buy it." So I said, "Okay, I'll try the new technology."

Actress Donna Mills and Ed were the first people in L.A. to get a Prius. We were the guinea pigs. And I love it. I'm so happy with it. It's a fabulous car.

I *hate* pumping gas. I just loathe it. Now I hardly ever have to. The hybrid is so dependable, too. It's quiet, it's fun, and it's easy to steer. It's very roomy inside, but small enough that it's very easy to maneuver.

Ed doesn't preach to people about being green. He doesn't walk into anyone's house and say, "You know, you could be a little bit better about recycling."

***He* doesn't. *I* do that. It's a flaw, a character defect. If I have to make sacrifices, you all have to make them, too. Misery loves company. But I don't consider driving a hybrid a sacrifice at all, so I**

cars produced in the United States were powered by electricity! **Most automobiles get better gas**

have no problem telling someone, "You gotta get rid of that car." We must have sold a hundred Priuses that way! By now a majority of our friends have some kind of eco-friendly car, or they're thinking about getting one.

The Prius really is a great car. It burns superclean and it works very well. So when I have to go beyond the range of the electric, I just take the hybrid. It can go 500 miles on a fill-up, easy, and I can fill it up like anyone in America, anywhere, with gasoline.

Hybrid Technology

There are several different ways to make a hybrid, but they all, whether a car or a truck, have some things in common. At least for now, they all have both a gasoline-powered internal-combustion engine, like most vehicles on the road, and an electric motor.

While most cars waste 25 percent of their gasoline when they're just idling, the gasoline engine in a hybrid shuts off when the car's stopped. This not only reduces fuel consumption dramatically, both around town and in highway traffic, but also reduces emissions dramatically.

Some hybrids can also run on the electric motor exclusively when coasting and when traveling at slow speeds, like in stop-and-go traffic or coming down a steep hill. The Prius falls into this category, as does the hybrid version of the Ford Escape, the Toyota Highlander, and the Lexus RX 400h (*h* is for hybrid). Under these conditions, the hybrid is just as clean as an electric car—and you don't have to worry about charging it.

That's because hybrid cars make their own electricity. Today's hybrids don't ever have to be plugged in to recharge. For one thing, hybrid cars—like those electric cars we talked about earlier—use regenerative braking to recharge the batteries that power the electric motor. Basically, when you hit the brakes, the electric motor applies resistance to the car's drivetrain, which makes the

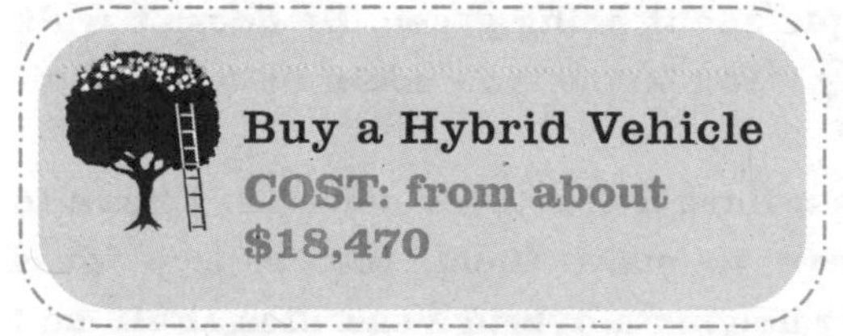

mileage on the highway than they do in city driving, but some hybrid cars get better mileage

wheels spin more slowly. The energy from the wheels then turns the electric motor, which acts like a generator, converting energy that is normally wasted in a car—when you're coasting, when you're braking—into electricity. That electricity gets stored in the car's battery until it's needed by the electric motor. The gasoline engine also charges the battery while you're driving (much as it does in a gasoline-only car).

Some hybrids engage both the electric motor and the gasoline engine at the same time. They use the electric motor to provide more power—when you're accelerating, when you're passing, and when you're climbing a hill—so then they can put a smaller, more efficient gasoline engine into the car. That helps to reduce emissions and improve gas mileage even further.

For instance:

- The 2007 Nissan Altima hybrid has Environmental Protection Agency (EPA) ratings of 42 mpg in the city and 36 mpg on the highway.
- The 2007 Toyota Prius is rated at 60 mpg city, 51 mpg highway.
- The 2007 Toyota Camry hybrid is rated at 40 city, 38 highway.
- The front-wheel-drive version of the 2007 Ford Escape hybrid is rated at 39 mpg city, 31 highway.
- And the 2007 Lexus RX 400h is rated at 32 mpg city (31 for the four-wheel-drive version), 27 mpg highway.

Now, as you probably noticed, not every hybrid was designed to get incredible gas mileage. Some are larger, like the sport utility vehicles, and they were designed to provide a sort of "best of both worlds" alternative: the ability to haul stuff and still have a more environmentally sound vehicle.

If they don't get phenomenal gas mileage, how can people say they're more environmentally sound? Because what comes out of the tailpipe is cleaner. In many cases, these vehicles have far lower emissions than an internal-combustion-engine vehicle that gets the same mileage numbers.

According to the EPA, the expected greenhouse gas emissions from a front-wheel-drive Ford Escape hybrid are just 5.4 tons per year—compared with 14.9 tons for the highest polluters on the market right now. And that figure for the Prius is just 3.4 tons. That's a dramatic difference.

in the city than they do on the highway. If you commute locally or in stop-and-go traffic,

I've also found that the maintenance costs—and needs—are largely reduced on hybrids. I'll only speak to Toyota, because those are the hybrids I've been driving for seven years. In those seven years, after racking up 130,000 miles, all the car has needed is a lube and oil change, and the routine scheduled maintenance at 50,000 miles and at 75,000. I've never had any other car that made it to 130,000 miles with my only investment being the lube and oil changes plus a $700 bill at 50,000 miles and maybe an $800 bill at 75,000 miles.

So these hybrids are multifaceted beauties. It's not just the emissions. It's the mileage, and it's the carefree maintenance. And then compared with electric vehicles, there's also the advantage of unlimited range.

Alternative Fuels

Beyond electric cars and hybrids, you've got other choices that are generally considered greener than regular gasoline-powered internal-combustion-engine vehicles. Alternative-fuel vehicles are squarely in this camp.

What exactly are alternative fuels? They're as follows:

- natural gas, in the form of compressed natural gas (CNG) or liquefied natural gas (LNG)
- propane, also called liquefied petroleum gas (LPG)
- biodiesel
- ethanol blends

Someday, *hydrogen* also might be a viable alternative fuel. It burns extremely clean. And it's the fuel that will be used in fuel cell cars, a type of technology that the government and automakers are investing in heavily, though its use in vehicles you and I can drive is probably several years away. A fuel cell is an electrochemical energy conversion device that mixes hydrogen and oxygen to make water, creating electricity in the process. The big drawback with hydrogen—and the reason I'm not a huge supporter of hydrogen fuel cell vehicles at this time—is that hydrogen is made by burning fossil fuels, so the benefits aren't enough to outweigh the drawbacks right now. We need to find a clean way to "make" hydrogen for it to be a fully green solution.

that's a real benefit. Why use perfectly good corn that could feed people here and in other

In the meantime, you *can* get a car today that burns one of these other alternative fuels. And if you can get around and do the tasks you need to do while you're burning one of these other fuels—while you're burning natural gas or propane or biodiesel or ethanol—it's often better for the environment than burning gasoline in a regular internal-combustion-engine car.

You may also qualify for some tax benefits, or be able to drive alone and still use the carpool lane. In California, you have to get a special sticker for your vehicle that will allow you to use the high-occupancy vehicle, or HOV, lane. Anyone who has dealt with L.A. traffic knows this can be a very big benefit indeed.

So let's take a quick look at each of these other alternative fuels and see what your options are today.

Natural Gas

Natural gas *is* a fossil fuel, but it's one of the cleanest-burning alternative fuels. Also, it's made primarily from methane. Furthermore, almost 87 percent of the natural gas used in the United States is *produced* right here in the U.S., so switching from a gasoline-powered car to a natural gas car helps reduce our dependence on foreign oil.

Consumers don't have many choices when it comes to shopping for a natural gas–powered car. In 2007 only one vehicle that ran exclusively on natural gas was available to consumers in the United States (as opposed to governments or big companies for their fleets). Actually, it was being sold only in California and New York. That vehicle is the Honda Civic GX NGV (for natural gas vehicle). It comes with a device called Phill, a refueling appliance that you connect to your home's gas line, the same type of gas line that fuels your stove or your clothes dryer. That way, you can fuel the car at home overnight, which makes it just as convenient as an electric car. A full tank gives you a range of 220 to 240 miles, so you can go pretty far with it, and if you use it around town, you will never have to go to a filling station.

Another option, when it comes to natural gas, is a flex-fuel vehicle, one that can run on natural gas and that can also run on either gasoline or diesel fuel. As the name suggests, a flex-fuel vehicle gives you more flexibility, since you can run on readily available gasoline or diesel when you can't find a natural gas filling station—and they're not easy to find as of yet.

RACHELLE'S TURN

We had some, um, adventures with a flex-fuel car that Ed used to own, which ran on natural gas and gasoline. We traveled cross-country in that car one time, and Ed had this old map of all the natural-gas filling stations. Now, they don't have an infrastructure for this stuff. It doesn't exist. We'd go to these places where there's supposed to be a tank of natural gas, and they'd be like, "Oh, no, three years ago they got rid of that."

But Ed was determined that he would find natural gas. So he would drive around for an hour in a city—burning natural gas while looking for natural gas—instead of just going to a gas station and filling up with gasoline until we could get to the next natural gas station.

On more than one occasion, we would go to a place and it would just be a stump. And then we'd be in the boondocks with not enough gas. And I would always be on pins and needles, wondering if we were going to make it across the country. It was never dull. But I did it once. One time. That was it.

Oh, and remember how I wouldn't take the electric car to the hospital when I was in labor with Hayden? Well, that meant we had to take the *other* car, which was this same natural gas flex-fuel car. So we get in, and we go out of the driveway toward the street, and Ed takes a left, and that's a funny way to go, because the hospital is in the other direction. Then he gets on the freeway and heads completely in the opposite direction. I asked, "Where are we going?" And Ed says, "We're out of natural gas, so we have to go to Glendale." Now, we live in Studio City,

waste into biodiesel fuel. **According to the National Resources Defense Council, the use of**

and Glendale is a good 10 miles away by freeway, so I was like "No way! Pull the car over! Get off the freeway! Get to a gas station immediately!"

I think he thought I was going to deliver right then and there, so he pulled off and went to a gas station, but even then he would not get out of the car and pump the gasoline. So I had to get out of the car—in labor—and pump gasoline. And I said, "I hope someone's taking your picture right now."

We finally made it to the hospital, with time to spare, but you never know about these things. My feeling is, get natural gas on your own time, buddy! Not when I'm in labor.

I'm not sure our marriage could have survived all this craziness for too many years. Thank goodness the car companies have come out with some really good green vehicles that are easy to live with, like my Prius and Ed's Phoenix SUT.

Well, Rachelle may be a bit dramatic about all this, but she does bring up a good point. If you're determined to use the greener fuel and avoid using gasoline, then a natural gas flex-fuel vehicle probably is not your best choice.

Natural gas does have some distinct advantages, though:

- It emits 60 to 90 percent less smog-producing pollutants than gasoline.
- It emits 30 to 40 percent less greenhouse gases.
- It's less expensive than gasoline.

However, natural gas intrinsically has less energy than gasoline, and that means you can't travel as far on a single tank of fuel. Also, flex-fuel vehicles have to have two separate fuel tanks (one for gasoline or diesel and the other for natural gas), so that cuts into your cargo-carrying space.

Propane

Propane is another clean-burning fossil fuel. Like natural gas, it's still a limited resource, but, again, it comes primarily from domestic sources—85 percent of the time. A propane-powered vehicle—such as a forklift or a

biofuels—especially cellulosic biofuels—could reduce our annual greenhouse gas emissions

propane-powered personal vehicle—runs much cleaner than one powered by gasoline. Propane is derived from crude oil, so it's not as environmentally friendly in many ways as other alternative fuels. But it is definitely cleaner. Vehicles powered by propane produce fewer toxic and smog-forming emissions, and liquefied petroleum gas (LPG) is less expensive than gasoline.

You can retrofit a gasoline or diesel vehicle to burn LPG—or to burn natural gas, for that matter. And propane is relatively easy to find. You just go to the same place you would go to refill the propane tank for your barbecue or your space heater.

For a while, no one was offering a vehicle that operated solely on propane. Then a company called Roush, a supplier to the automakers that has a long-standing relationship with Ford, introduced the 2007.5 Roush Ford F-150. It's got a liquid propane injection (LPI) system. Roush converts a Ford F-150 pickup with the 5.4-liter Triton V-8 engine to run on propane, and the truck's got the same horsepower and torque ratings as the gas version. You even order it and have it serviced at a Ford dealer. So it should be about as easy to live with as the gas-powered version of this truck, while reducing emissions.

Get Powered by Propane

COST: from about $25,945 (MSRP)

Biodiesel

Traditional diesel fuel has been a big problem. What we've suspected for years—what your nose and lungs tell you, what your breathing apparatus tells you—is that diesel emissions are very bad for your health. And now that's been proven.

The problem is the particulate matter (PM) that comes out of a diesel vehicle's tailpipe. The allowable threshold for this sooty matter has changed. Once upon a time it could be up to PM 10; that's 10 microns in size. Now nothing over 2½ microns is allowed, and it's a fraction of the width of a human hair. Still, diesel exhaust has a lot of PM 2.5, and these little particles are very damaging to your lungs. Because they're so small, they get in there really deep and really far.

by 1.7 billion tons by the year 2050. That's more than 80 percent of our current transportation-

Clean diesel has a lot less sulfur in it than traditional diesel fuel, and that's a step in the right direction. Still, we've long viewed "clean diesel" as an oxymoron, because even the clean diesel is made from traditional crude oil products, so it's just not as clean as so many other things available today, including natural gas. Electric cars are much cleaner, as are hybrids.

However, there is something called *biodiesel* that's cleaner than clean diesel—and, more important, it's not refined from crude oil, like regular diesel fuel. Biodiesel is made from vegetable oils, animal fats, or recycled restaurant greases. You can even take vegetable oil, refine it slightly in your garage, and then run your car on it. That burns pretty clean.

But keep in mind, on the plus and minus sides, even biodiesel emissions have some PM 2.5 and NOx, that is to say, oxides of nitrogen in it. If it's made from vegetable oil, I imagine it's less harmful than crude oil particles, but the exhaust still contains particulate matter that's not good for your lungs. Simply stated, the tailpipe of a hybrid is cleaner than the tailpipe of a biodiesel car.

The reason I mentioned biodiesel at all is because it's not a refined product coming from crude oil. There're none of the challenges that we get with Mideast oil and all the many forms of pollution that come from drilling and what have you. But I'm not strongly in favor of biodiesel either, because there's an energy stream that's involved in making biodiesel. It's made from *new* corn and *new* soybeans, which are harvested with lots of John Deere equipment, which may or may not run on biodiesel. All the equipment used to harvest the crops—and all the fossil fuels used to make the fertilizers to grow the corn and the soybeans—tax the environment, too. Now, biodiesel can be good for U.S. farmers—it's a great cash crop for them—and I want to support the farmers just like Willie Nelson does. I want clean fuel, and I want to help the farmers, too. But maybe we can help the farmers in other ways, by making biodiesel from AG (agricultural) waste. Grow the corn to feed *people,* and what have you got left? A big old cornstalk, a huge stalk with lots of cel-

related emissions. Since 40 percent of all car trips are 2 miles or less, it's really easy to

lulose in it that can be turned into biodiesel. Lots of other crops have AG waste that can be used to make biodiesel, too. It's another win-win.

Maybe we also can help farmers by having them plant switchgrass, which is so easy to grow, it grows wild. If we can make the biodiesel from switchgrass or from AG waste, then I'm really in favor of it. It's much more desirable economically, environmentally, in every way.

Even as is, biodiesel is biodegradable and nontoxic, so if it does spill, it doesn't require a hazardous waste cleanup program.

In short, biodiesel has great promise. And can they clean up the problem with oxides of nitrogen in biodiesel exhaust? Absolutely. Can they clean up the problems with PM 2.5 in biodiesel? No question. And they should right away, because that's something you can address with a particulate trap—an existing technology.

You can use biodiesel in its pure form, 100 percent biodiesel, also called B100. But few people do. The people who manufacture biodiesel usually blend it with petroleum diesel. The most common blends are B2 (2 percent biodiesel), B5, and B20.

Most vehicle manufacturers *do not* recommend using blends greater than 5 percent. In fact, using a higher blend will void some engine warranties. Car companies generally do say that B2 and B5 can be used safely in most diesel engines.

Ethanol Blends

Ethanol is a type of alcohol, like methanol. It's made by fermenting and distilling starch crops, like corn—or what's known as *cellulosic biomass,* like trees and grasses—so it's similar to biodiesel in terms of what it's made of, and it too is made domestically. It burns very clean—reducing greenhouse gas emissions—and because you're using that much less fossil fuel, you're again reducing dependence on foreign oil.

But while biodiesel can be used only in a diesel engine, *some* ethanol can be used in any gasoline engine—and there are far more gasoline-engine vehicles on the road today than there are diesels, especially in the United States. All of the car companies have approved the use of E10—also called *gasohol*—in their cars and trucks. E10 is a blend made of 10 percent ethanol

make the change from driving to biking. Currently, there are no alternative fuels for airplanes,

and 90 percent gasoline, so running E10 will not affect your vehicle's warranty. It's okay to use it in any gas-powered car or truck. That alone makes ethanol a desirable alternative fuel, since it's usable, at least to a degree, in so many vehicles.

Many vehicles on the road right now are also designed to run on a blend called E85, which is 85 percent ethanol and 15 percent gasoline. Most of these vehicles are flex-fuel vehicles, so you can run them on E85, on gasoline, or on any combination of the two.

The only real drawback to these flex-fuel vehicles is that their engine management computers haven't been programmed to run exclusively on E85. That means your gas mileage could drop as much as 25 percent when you run E85 instead of gas, because ethanol has a lower energy content than gasoline.

On the plus side, E85 is cheaper than gasoline, especially in the Midwest. And because it has a higher octane content, you may experience more power from your engine by running E85. (If your car has a problem with pinging, or detonation, it may also benefit by running some ethanol.) Unfortunately, it's not the easiest fuel to find, but there are several hundred filling stations selling E85 across the country. It's the chicken-and-the-egg thing. The reason they are not making great quantities of the fuel and not many stations sell it is because they figure, "There's not many cars that run on it. We're not gonna put up any stations." Now that several automakers, including GM, are making flex-fuel vehicles that run on E85, I'm sure we'll start to see more stations that sell E85.

To Fly or Not to Fly

At the very bottom of my transportation hierarchy—and with good reason—is air travel. Simply put, I'd rather not fly. It's not that I'm afraid. Statistically, it's safer in the sky than it is on a highway. I just don't like to fly at 31,000 feet burning kerosene.

That's right, that's what jet fuel is: kerosene with a mold retardant. When it's burned, it emits all these pollutants:

- carbon dioxide (CO_2), which is a leading cause of global warming
- oxides of nitrogen

but they could conceivably run on biofuels someday. One round-trip flight from the United

• sulfur dioxide
• soot
• water vapor

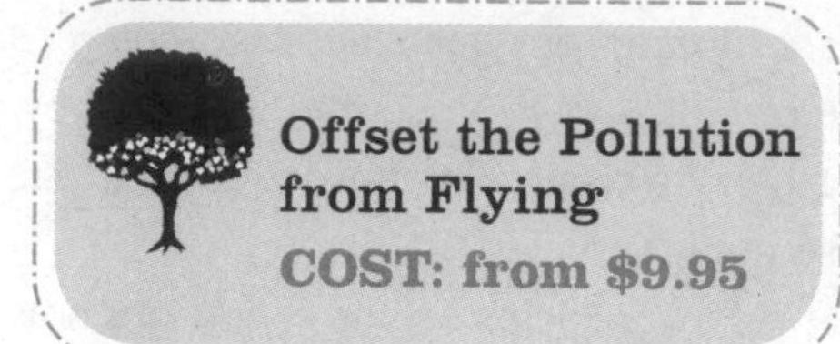

Emitting all that CO_2 is bad enough, but experts say the cocktail created by those other emissions may double airplanes' total impact on climate change.

And unlike pollution created at street level, there are no trees up in the stratosphere to mitigate that CO_2, that pollution. What happens to it? How does it affect global climate change? Some studies suggest it could be quite damaging.

Mile for mile, driving a very clean hybrid—with its low tailpipe emissions—just plain creates less pollutants in the air than your share of that plane ride will.

The mileage is not *bad* when you fly, if you're in one of the more efficient planes, and if you take off and land without a lot of circling. You can get 50-some-odd miles per gallon. But you're burning kerosene. And you've seen jets. When you're behind a jet, the exhaust smells a little different from what comes out of a hybrid car.

Sure, there are a lot of people on an airplane. But compare it to a Greyhound bus. A Greyhound bus runs on diesel fuel, usually, and when you average it out, it gets about 400 mpg, because there are usually seventy-some-odd people on it. You're getting really good mileage, given the relatively light weight of a Greyhound bus and the relatively small amount of fuel it consumes per passenger. Jet engines burn through a lot more fuel, so even when they're full, their mileage is nowhere near as good—just 50 to 60 mpg. And again, they're burning kerosene.

So I only fly when I must. If at all possible I'd much rather drive the hybrid than fly.

RACHELLE'S TURN

The most challenging part of living with Ed has been adjusting to his transportation issues. It's gotten better, since we have hybrids and better electric cars and better cars in general—even the gasoline-burning cars are much cleaner.

States to Europe will add 3 to 4 tons to your carbon footprint. **According to the Tyndall Centre**

But someone gave Ed grief once while he was waiting to board a plane: "Oh, some environmentalist you are. Flying in an airplane," and now there's no flying anymore. We got invited to these elaborate four-day weekend trips to Venice with all of Hollywood, all expenses paid. The invitations alone were so beautiful you wanted to frame them. But no, can't go. And inside I was thinking, "Oh, I hate you so much. I just hate you."

Another time, we got invited to Alaska, and Ed was going to *drive* there. But he had just had his femur reset from an accident, and the doctors said, "If you drive, you will be crippled for the rest of your life." So I got a campaign of people to call Ed and say, "You know, you should probably see what you're preserving once before it changes," because he had never been to Alaska. We got to go on that trip, but not without a lot of, ahem, persuasion.

I *like* to drive. I like the highway, the solitude, the peace, the changing scenery. And if I get from L.A. to Vancouver for $90, I'm laughing. When I have to go on a trip for an acting job, I'll call up the production company and say, "How much will you reimburse me for the airfare? $830? You mind if I drive? Will you give me the money?" So they give me $830 and it cost me $180 round-trip, and I'm $650 in the black before I've said a single line of dialogue.

I'll drive to New York. I'll drive to Philadelphia. I'd prefer to drive anywhere, rather than fly, if I've got the time. And I can usually make the time.

RACHELLE'S TURN

I drove cross-country with Ed a couple of times. Most people do that once in a lifetime, right? But no, that's a pretty common occurrence for Ed.

Me, I fly. I figure the plane's going there anyway. It's not like I like to fly, and I'm not jumping on a plane all the time. Actually, I really *don't* like to fly. That shows you how much I *really* don't like to drive. It's too boring. Maybe if Ed let me drive, I'd have a little more interest. And he never goes above the speed limit, 55 or 65 all the way. It's absolute torture.

So we've worked out a compromise: One drives, one flies. Whatever it takes to make it all work, you know. He might be a

for Climate Change Research at the University of Manchester, CO_2 emissions from airplane

little tired when he gets where we're going, but at least he knows where his luggage is. He does take steps to offset the pollution whenever I fly—or on those rare occasions when I'm able to get him on a plane.

When I do have to fly—or when Rachelle chooses to fly—there's something I do to mitigate the CO_2 footprint, the carbon footprint, from all that kerosene being burned at 31,000 feet. What I do is I get a TerraPass flight tag. I'll let my friend Adam Stein from TerraPass explain what a carbon footprint is and how TerraPass offsets it.

Ed's Green Friend: TerraPass

Climate change is a global problem with a local cause. Almost everything we do requires energy in one form or another. And that energy, more often than not, comes from fossil fuels.

It's possible for each of us to quantify our own contribution to global warming. We all have a ***carbon footprint,*** named after carbon dioxide, the principal greenhouse gas responsible for climate change. Your carbon footprint is the total of all the greenhouse gas emissions caused by your daily activities.

Driving is one source of greenhouse gas emissions, but it isn't the only one. Most likely your home uses just as much energy as your car. Heating your house and keeping the lights on has just as much impact as driving.

Another big source of greenhouse gas emissions is plane travel. Flying is fast, cheap, and polluting. A round-trip flight between New York and Los Angeles burns about 100 gallons of kerosene ***per passenger.***

TerraPass allows you to use ***carbon offsets*** to lighten your climate change footprint.

What is a carbon offset? Although a complex topic, it is a simple thing. A carbon offset represents the reduction of one ton of carbon dioxide emissions. When you buy an offset, you fund that reduction in emissions.

Carbon offsets typically come from clean energy or efficiency projects. For example, wind farms create clean electricity that displaces electricity from coal. A utility company receives power from a wind farm, so it can produce that much less power by burning coal. The result is a reduction in carbon dioxide emissions. Wind farms generate clean electricity. They also generate carbon offsets.

The important feature of high-quality carbon offsets is that they represent reductions in greenhouse gas emissions that would not have happened otherwise. High-quality carbon offsets are a means of hastening our transition to a clean energy infrastructure. High-quality offset vendors, such as TerraPass, use a variety of verification techniques, including independent audits, to ensure that the offsets have the intended effect.

There are lots of things you can do to lower your energy use. But you can't reduce your energy use to zero, which is where carbon offsets come into play. You can use carbon offsets to balance out the emissions you can't eliminate through personal conservation.

Ed is a perfect example. His personal carbon footprint is very low, because he generates his own solar electricity and drives an electric car. But for longer trips, he drives a hybrid car, which runs on gasoline. And for really long trips, he and Rachelle fly.

To balance out the emissions from these activities, Ed buys a TerraPass. TerraPass makes products designed to balance emissions from driving, flying, and home energy use. By purchasing a TerraPass, Ed funds verified reductions in greenhouse gas emissions so that he can travel carbon-balanced. More important, he helps move us a little further down the road toward clean energy.

—Adam Stein

Essentially, TerraPass goes to the marketplace and buys new clean power—solar power, wind power, something that does not emit CO_2—then that clean power gets fed into the grid, augmenting what is created by utility companies.

Maybe you're thinking, "That's kind of a feel-good thing, but is it really doing anything?"

Let me be clear: It does not negate the real pollution created from a tailpipe of a car or from somebody's home energy use or from air travel. That's real. That's out there. You're not taking that away. But neither are you taking away the green power that they're putting in the system. That's real, too. And over time, that could balance out and account for the closure of power plants. At some point, they'll be shutting down coal plants because they have sufficient power coming from clean sources. (We'll go into this more in Chapter 4, "Energy.") If every air passenger bought a TerraPass each time he or she flew, it would be a very real contribution to creating greener energy for all of us.

TerraPass is the best way I have found to mitigate my carbon footprint, and the company makes it very easy. For a plane flight, you just go online to TerraPass.com, log on, and enter your miles traveled and how many people are traveling. You can then buy a TerraPass to balance the emissions for your level of energy use. You can also buy a yearly TerraPass, if you just want to give an estimate to make things easy so you're not doing it every trip. And it's very inexpensive, something like $7 for the last airplane trip we took.

So far, 40,000 people have bought TerraPasses, so that's a lot of green energy fed into the system, a lot of very real offsets that have occurred. Imagine if 400,000 people did it. If four million people did it. Everybody would take notice then.

A TerraPass for Your Car

Maybe you can't go out and buy an electric car or a hybrid or an alternative-fuel vehicle right now. You don't have the money at the moment, or maybe you really love the car you have. You can still make a real difference, environmentally speaking, by purchasing a TerraPass for your car.

They're going to ask you, "How many miles do you drive annually?" All you do is see what it says on your odometer and—unless you had some extraordinary big year of driving, or big year of not driving—divide that number by the amount of years since you bought the car, if you bought it new. (If you bought it used, look at the receipt and see how many miles it had when you purchased it, then deduct that from the total on the odometer before you average out your annual mileage.)

Next, you select your car model from the list on the website, and it will tell you what size TerraPass you need to mitigate the amount of CO_2 you put out in a year's worth of driving.

travel in Britain will surpass those from automobile travel in the next five to seven years.

I mostly drive my electric car, but I do drive cross-country in the hybrid sometimes, so I computed that amount for my cross-country drives. For a Prius, for 10,000 miles a year, it was less than $40. It wasn't a lot of money, and I feel good about it.

It's All About Choices

Every day, you have choices—probably even more than you realize. You can get in your car and drive to a store that's three blocks away or you can walk there. You can ride your bike there. You can get some exercise and reduce pollution and reduce traffic congestion at the same time—or not. Your call.

If you have to go farther than you can comfortably walk or bike, you can choose public transportation if that is an option where you live. You can take a train or a bus or the subway. Again, it's a chance for you to reduce traffic congestion and reduce pollution and multitask, too. You can get some work done or read a book while you ride.

When you do have to drive—say it's 40 degrees below zero outside or you have to go someplace that you can't reach by public transportation or you can't get there quickly enough by bus or by train—you still have other choices. You can drive an electric car or you can drive a hybrid or you can drive an alternative-fuel vehicle. You also can get a TerraPass, make one choice—one easy choice for very little money—and make a genuine difference, no matter what you drive. And the same goes for those times when you have to fly.

It's all about choices, and none of them are painful. They're not going to make you suffer—regardless of what my wife might say. Often it's quite the opposite. Often, these choices will make you *feel* good while you *do* something good.

Which brings us to another series of feel-good, do-good choices: choices about what to do with your trash, with your waste. And the short answer is: Recycle.

Driving a hybrid can reduce global-warming pollutants by one-third to one-half.

midnight!
YOUR
TAX

RECYCLING

OLD BECOMES NEW

3

Nearly everything can be recycled—or reused, which is another wonderful form of recycling. There's value in just about everything, even that tattered old throw rug. Groups like Freecycle find new uses for old, cast-off items. If you tell members, "I've got an old throw rug that's tattered," someone may know somebody who can use it. A rescue pet clinic might need something for the dogs to lie around on, for example.

So let's start with the basics, a sort of Recycling 101, before we get into more detail about how you can recycle and reuse all kinds of different stuff.

RACHELLE'S TURN

Recycling is Ed's life. It's his passion.

When we first decided to move in together, I realized I was going to have to embrace recycling. Every single thing I wanted to dispose of would have to be considered. Could it be recycled? If so, which bin did it go in? (He had a ridiculous number of bins and still does!)

I learned that just about everything you own can be recycled, and my lifestyle had to reflect that. Today, if I want to make a change around the house, that change has to involve recycling. I can put a new rug in my Pilates studio—as long as it's my old living room rug, cleaned and reused. But what do I do with the nasty old rug that was in the Pilates studio? Ed wanted to give it to Goodwill. But who wants a torn-up old rug?

Eventually, Ed agreed, but he still said, "If anyone thinks this is going in a landfill, they're out of their mind. Maybe the fiber can be used for something. Fiber has value."

To Ed, everything is potentially something else. I never underestimate Ed when it comes to recycling. He'll always find a way.

Why Recycle?

Recycling is important for a number of reasons. First and foremost, there's energy to be saved in most recycling programs, aluminum being at the head of the class, the top of the heap.

When you think about it, just back-of-the-envelope calculation will bring you to the same point that every study does: It takes so much less energy to mine our aluminum on our street corners and in our alleys and at our recycling centers than it does to travel to Jamaica, use large John Deere or Caterpillar equipment to mine bauxite, to refine the ore, to take it to a smelter, to bring it to the United States, and to fabricate it into a can. That's a number—all that work and all that energy is a number. Now, what's the other number, to have curbside recycling bins and recycling centers all across the country, where you can mine the very pure form of bauxite known as aluminum and use a minimal amount of energy to make that into a new can?

When an aluminum can gets recycled and made into a new can, it can wind up back on a

Another very important point: The idea of using these perfectly wonderful resources—be they petroleum, bauxite, or any other resource—to make different things, then to throw those things in this big toxic soup known as a landfill, only to have to go get *more* resources and use *them* up is crazy to me. Recycling saves a tremendous amount of natural resources.

Landfills

The other issue is: Where does all this stuff go?

"Honey, throw that away." "Sweetie, can you throw this away for me?"

Where is *away*? *Away* is just someone else's backyard.

Landfills serve us the way the portrait served Dorian Gray. They allow us to cavort in an orgy of consumerism until the final day of reckoning—which is yesterday or today, depending on where you live.

You can call a landfill other things. They call it a *sanitary landfill.* They call it a *dump*—a more appropriate name, I suppose, because people want to just dump stuff on someone else and sweep it under the rug.

But it ultimately doesn't do a very good job. All landfills leak. It's not just solid matter that's thrown in a landfill. There are liquids, too, and a lot of them are toxic. Rightly or wrongly, people do throw toxic substances in a landfill. I say "rightly or wrongly," but of course it's very wrong. That's why there are hazardous waste drop-off sites and hazardous waste pickup days. People should take advantage of that, but do they? Absolutely not. Sadly, they throw their half-used can of cleaning solution, the old can of paint they don't need anymore, their batteries, their old computer monitor, right into a trash can, where it is picked up and mixed together with all the other allowable waste and sent off to a landfill.

What happens next? It rains. Of course, the people who build and manage landfills are very careful. They put a cap on the top of the landfill, or a liner, to keep the rain out.

A liner is just a big sheet of plastic, and, of course, plastic leaks. The rain will eventually get down into the landfill.

grocery store shelf in just 90 days. Now that's efficient. **A landfill is a place to sweep waste**

But wait, isn't there another liner on the bottom of the landfill, so it won't leach on down into the water table below? Sure there is, but when you've got all these sharp objects in a landfill, they cut or tear holes in the plastic. So the liquids are able to seep out of the landfill and into the earth below.

Any landfill is essentially a big bathtub in the ground. And as any plumber will tell you, all bathtubs will eventually leak. Some liquid will eventually get through.

Gravity always wins, even with matter in a solid state. How quickly do you think it wins with matter in a liquid state? Over time, toxic substances will leach into your water table—the same water beneath the earth's surface that supplies wells and springs. The water that we drink and swim in. The water that fish and other sea creatures live in. Hmm, I wonder if that's a good idea.

You need only travel to the Fresh Kills landfill on Staten Island in New York City—or any landfill in America—to see all the birds circling overhead. Circling. Landing. Feeding on the toxic elements in the landfill. And, with great regularity, getting snared on the plastic rings from six-packs. Ingesting all of those Styrofoam peanuts, all of those different plastics. Many different species are adversely affected by landfills because of the toxins and the ubiquitous presence of plastics that harm them in so many ways.

The Landfill Siting Issue

There've been landfills for thousands of years. In the earliest settlements of man, you can find midden mounds, which are basically landfills. There's detritus. There's trash left over from former civilizations.

When there were one billion of us on the planet, we could seemingly act with impunity as there was plenty of space to dump our trash. Now that our planet is more crowded, people have started to complain, rightly, about the landfill near their home, the odor from the landfill, the vermin that congregate around the landfill.

In days gone by we enjoyed the *illusion* of disposal, of throwing things away and having them just disappear, or cease to exist. In the West, there was so much space, it was possible to site landfills out of sight, out of mind. People on the East Coast, by no small coincidence, understood that this illu-

conveniently under the rug. Another sad side effect of landfills is their impact on wildlife.

sion was in fact false much sooner than the rest of the country because the East is far more densely settled. In the '80s, an orphan garbage barge from Islip, New York, created an uproar when the residents of Nassau County, Long Island, couldn't get another municipality to accept their garbage. So the people with the garbage decided they'd take it somewhere else. And *those* people wouldn't take it. They tried another place and got the same story. That barge made a 6,000-mile journey before they found somewhere to dump the load.

And all this played out in front of us, thanks to the media, and it woke us up to the question of where this stuff goes. People got to thinking, "Would I want a landfill in *my* backyard?" I sure don't. Do you?

All that attention to landfill siting and the overabundance of garbage gave recycling a big boost. More and more states came on board with recycling bills and instituted deposits on containers. And it's continued to grow since then due in large part to landfill siting concerns.

The Economics of Trash

Despite the fact that no one wants trash, there's a lot of money in it. It's big business. For years, organized crime had a tremendous presence in the waste-hauling industry. It's my understanding that that's changed, and I hope that's the case. But there are some very big waste haulers who, for years, were opposed to recycling programs because they felt it encroached on their business.

Some of these waste-hauling companies have gotten into the recycling business in a big way themselves because they've come to realize there's money to be made there.

The unfortunate side effect of this is that many of the smaller recycling firms, the mom-and-pop firms, have been driven out of business, and that's very sad.

There's another side to the economics of trash, too:

Many things—from the sun visor in your car to the screen

Nowadays, it's cheaper to replace a lot of things than it is to repair them. Today, there are

door on your house—are made as a unit. If part of it breaks, you're expected to replace the whole thing; you can't just change the mirror in the sun visor. And there's no easy way to replace the screen mesh in a new screen door. So people are being encouraged to throw away things that likely would not have been thrown away a short time ago. That makes for more trash. But it also creates more opportunities for recycling, including many of those we're about to discuss.

Curbside Recycling Programs

Fortunately, many cities across the United States have a curbside recycling program. These include many smaller municipalities and suburban areas, as well as large locales including:

- Boston
- Houston
- San Antonio
- Portland (Maine, Oregon, *and* Tennessee)
- Grand Rapids
- New York City
- Kansas City
- Salt Lake City
- San Diego
- Albuquerque

These curbside programs have vastly increased the amount of material coming into the MRFs, or materials recovery facilities. That's material that doesn't go to a landfill, so these programs can be a huge boon in many ways.

But there has been criticism about the pollution created *by* these recycling programs. That is to say: trucks—diesel trucks, in many cities—driving around and picking up this material. "For what?" critics say. "So people can feel warm and fuzzy about recycling?"

I will concede there is a certain amount of pollution involved in collecting recyclables. Critics also say that there's a lot of energy used and—in their opinion—wasted on these curbside pickup programs. In my opinion, it takes

nearly nine thousand curbside recycling programs across the United States. And as a nation,

a lot less energy to mine this stuff in our alleys and on our street corners than to mine new raw materials at the source, and it also prevents more material from going into the landfills.

When you consider the low-hanging fruit, the most energy saved is by collecting and recycling aluminum. If you go back to the top of the pyramid—the amount of aluminum recycled vs. mined in Jamaica—it's still a beneficial trade-off.

Critics also argue—and they are correct—that there have been highly inefficient recycling programs that do not make a positive environmental contribution. They are operating at a net loss, an environmental deficit, by generating diesel fumes.

There's another challenge to making these programs environmentally viable: our urban miners. For years we in the recycling realm have praised those—our homeless and others who clearly are not homeless—who go around picking the gold (in this case aluminum) out of the recycling bins. When the recycling that's picked up by the town or city has already been cherry-picked of most of the valuable materials, the city can't get its redemption value—that is, the deposits you and I have paid on aluminum cans and glass bottles and other containers. The municipalities running these recycling programs count on that money. And suddenly, they're picking up mostly corrugated cardboard, and there's not as much money coming into the coffers to support the program. There's no money to be made in a curbside program from chipped cardboard (especially if it's contaminated with other waste), different papers, and glass containers. Deciding to reclaim these materials is a judgment call at best, because you're basically hauling around sand. That's all glass is made of. There may be a deposit on it, but sand is heavy, and it may not be as economically viable to recover as those aluminum cans.

For example, the city of Napa, California, estimates that urban miners—they call them *thieves*—"steal" as much as half a million dollars' worth of cans and deposit bottles a year. So they urge residents and business owners

we recycle 32 percent of our waste. While there may be inefficiencies in recycling programs,

to call a nonemergency hotline if they spot people going through their recycling bins. In Los Angeles County, you're supposed to call the sheriff's department, so these scavengers can be fined or even serve jail time.

Though I would not condone fines or jail terms for homeless folks trying to make a buck, I would suggest finding ways to make every recycling program more efficient *and* more cost effective.

SORTING YOUR TRASH

Whether or not your city has a curbside recycling program, you're still going to need to sort your trash. Even cities that don't have a curbside program usually have neighborhood drop-off locations where you can bring your recyclables. If you live in an apartment or a condo that doesn't have recycling bins, you can do the same. No matter how your trash gets to the recycling facility, the first step is always the same: sorting.

In many cities, it's been made pretty easy. The Department of Sanitation issues different-colored bins. In Los Angeles we have three:

- Black is for stuff that goes to the landfill.
- Green is for yard waste.
- Blue is for recycling.

We're lucky in that we can put most of our recyclable stuff in one bin, including several different kinds of plastic, aluminum cans, glass, even mixed paper. That's a lot of stuff. My blue bin is always topped off with recyclable materials.

In Brooklyn, New York, on the other hand, paper for recycling gets its own separate bin and pickup, while mixed glass, metal, and plastic go in another, and yard waste is not recycled at all except at certain designated times of the year. So it's important to check the local regulations carefully, and put *only* the items in your recycling bins that are designated on your bin or in the materials list issued by your municipality. You don't want to put things in there that shouldn't go there. Nor do

the solution is to make each and every recycling program more efficient. Just because some-you want to put in anything that's dirty—no cat food cans with cat food still inside—because it contaminates other materials. Putting the wrong stuff in the recycling bin just creates extra work, since the people at the recycling center wind up throwing that stuff away. You're literally making them spend more money to pick up and transport your trash, which makes a mess of the recycling program. So don't put stuff in the recycling bin that's not supposed to go there.

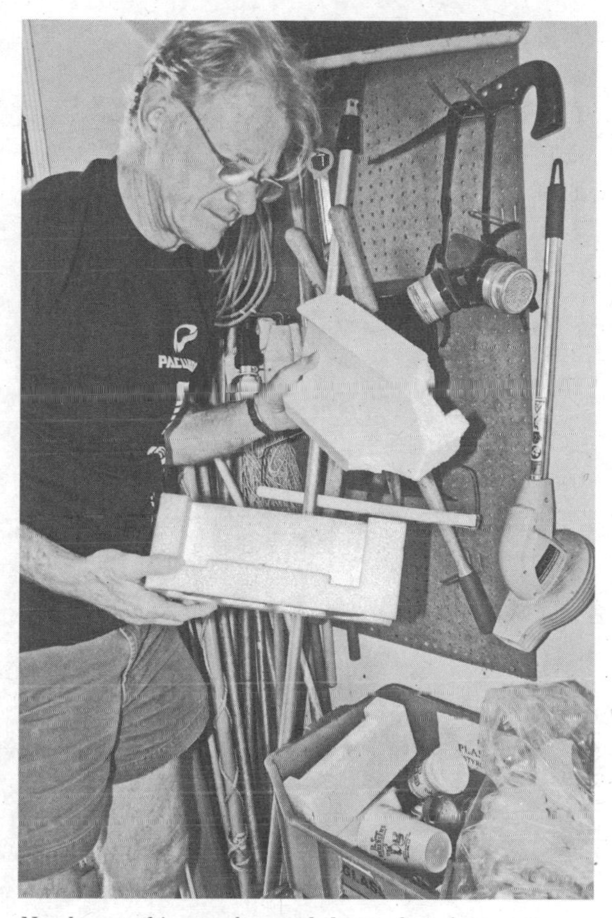

Nearly everything can be recycled, even Styrofoam.

As for the green bins, every week I have one or two filled with yard waste. The city does two things with all that stuff. One is a really good form of recycling; the other is only *kind* of recycling.

The good thing they do is they make something called L.A. Grow, a soil amendment. The plant material is put in a big drum grinder, and ground up and mixed with other things to make this very beneficial mulch, which is made available to L.A. residents.

Another way yard waste is used is not really *recycling* but it's still a fine use of this stuff at the landfill. Each time they lay out a layer of garbage, they cover it with a layer of green sediment. Another layer of garbage, another layer of green sediment. Otherwise, you just have rotting garbage and seagulls and a real mess, with the stench and the possibility of disease. Rather than waste good topsoil to cover each layer of garbage, which is what landfills used to do, now they can use green waste.

thing can't go in your curbside recycling bin doesn't mean it can't be recycled. All kinds of

What can't go into my compost bin gets chopped up and put in the green trash bin.

Of course, I don't put everything that *can* go in the green bin *into* the green bin. I recycle most of my own green waste—grass clippings, yard waste, and also table scraps—into compost (more on that in Chapter 5, "In the Garden and Kitchen"). So my green bins get stuff put in them only when it's not compostable, things I can't take a machete to and chop up. Even so, I fill one or two green bins with stuff every week, because it's a big property

resources make it possible to recycle *almost* everything. Recycling just one aluminum can

with lots of drought-tolerant plants and lots of shrubby stuff—things with thick branches and stalks that I can't compost.

What about the black bin, the stuff that goes to the landfill? On a weekly basis my black bin is usually one-eighth to one-quarter full. It's never even half filled. There's just not a lot of trash to be thrown out in this house. When I was single, there was even less—so little it would fit in my car's glove compartment! Now that there are more people with different habits living in the house, we do produce more trash, but still, we send very little to the landfill.

So what goes in our black bin? Things that simply cannot be recycled, like used kitty litter. You can't recycle or compost that. There also comes a point where you've gotta throw some things away. Things that Freecycle won't even take. When you've got a vegan tennis shoe that is tattered and the heel has come off and you've reglued it several times and it's now torn, nobody wants that. If you give this stuff to Goodwill, you're just making them work to throw *your* stuff away; they've got to pick it up and then pay the trash disposal cost to get rid of it. So be honest about what can be reused. Still, you'll find—as I have—that most things you want to get rid of have some value to someone. Empty soup cans, glass jars from pasta sauce, yesterday's newspaper—they all have value. So now let's look at these different kinds of materials and see how they can be recycled.

RECYCLING METAL

Obviously, there are many different kinds of metal—aluminum, steel, copper, gold, to name just a few—and most of them can be recycled.

You likely will have lots of aluminum to recycle, since 99 percent of all beer cans and 97 percent of all soft drink cans are made of aluminum.

Now, you may not want to put those cans in your curbside recycling bin, because many states offer a cash value for those empty cans. They're not really paying you, of course; they're just refunding your money. They charge something like a 5¢ deposit for each can when you buy a six-pack or a twelve-pack. Then when you bring

saves enough energy to run a television set for three hours. Steel recycling saves enough

the empty cans back, they refund your deposit. Either way—whether you collect the cash or throw the cans into your curbside recycling bin so your city can collect the cash—those aluminum cans will get recycled.

Fortunately, aluminum is easy to recycle. You don't have to remove any labels. You just rinse out the cans. When it's recycled, aluminum gets processed at such a high temperature that it easily eliminates contaminants. You rinse the stuff primarily to prevent odors and make life easier on all the people who have to touch that can after you're done with it—the people who sort all the stuff that goes in the recycling bin, and then later, the people at the plant that recycles the aluminum.

Where does that aluminum get reused? To make more cans, mostly.

What about steel? Believe it or not, more steel gets recycled each year than all other materials combined, including paper. This is due in part to the fact that you can attract steel with a magnet. So it's easy to sort it out when it's mixed in with other materials. Steel can be salvaged fairly easily even if it's mixed in with construction debris or debris from a demolished building. It might come out of a junked car or an old appliance.

Recycling that steel not only keeps it from going to a landfill, but also saves energy and natural resources. Every ton of steel that gets recycled reduces the need for 2,500 pounds of iron ore, 1,400 pounds of coal, and 120 pounds of limestone.

So what kinds of metal can go into curbside recycling bins? Obviously aluminum cans. Also other common household stuff, like clean aluminum foil, pie tins, tin cans, and jar lids (which should be put in separately from the jars).

If you have metal trash that can't go in your curbside recycling bin—anything from an old screen door to a cast-iron skillet—there are other recycling resources. There are scrap-metal yards all over the country, places that will even give you a little cash based on the quantity of the metal you bring in. Even precious metals like gold and silver can be recycled. They can literally be melted down to make new jewelry or new coins or what have you.

RECYCLING GLASS

Glass is one of the easiest materials to recycle. Every single glass food and drink container you get can be recycled. It may not be as valuable as aluminum, but it's still well worth the effort.

energy each year to provide a year's worth of electricity for about one-fifth of all U.S. house-

Again, you don't even have to remove the labels before you recycle glass containers. Just rinse them out. The high-temperature processing will remove any contaminants.

The important point about glass is that some types cannot be mixed together. You can't mix glass bottles with windows—car windows or building windows—or mirrors or glass dishes or drinking glasses or things like Pyrex kitchen bowls. You have to keep ceramic stuff separate, too, since it will contaminate glass. For the most part, that means you can put only glass bottles and jars in your curbside recycling bin.

What happens to the glass you send off for recycling? Odds are you will wind up buying it again. Most of the glass recycled in the United States gets used in new glass containers, though some of it is used to make fiberglass, too.

RECYCLING PLASTICS

RACHELLE'S TURN

When it comes to plastic, Ed knows more than anybody. There are seven different kinds of plastic, designated by seven different recycling numbers. I marvel at Ed's ability to retain all those numbers and what they mean. All I know is they put a recycling symbol on the bottom of all plastic stuff. In the middle of the symbol is a number. That number tells you if the thing can be recycled or not. I always have to turn things over and look at the number—and then ask Ed to figure out if it can go in the recycling bin.

We have blue bins for recycling and I think you can only put no. 1 and 2 plastic in the bins. I think no. 5 is not good, but maybe it's 6. I just can't remember.

In a city like L.A., until very recently, you could put only two kinds of plastic in the blue recycling bin, no. 1 and no. 2. You couldn't put no. 3, 4, 5, 6, or 7 plastic into the bin, but you still could recycle some of them.

The only things you couldn't recycle in this house were those made of resins no. 3 and no. 5. The plastics industry would say it's all recyclable, and I'm sure it is, but I don't live near a processing plant that takes it. Your town

holds. **Recycling just a single glass jar or bottle saves enough energy to light a standard 100-watt**

THE SEVEN KINDS OF PLASTIC

No. 1	Polyethylene terephthalate (PET)	This kind of plastic is used to make things like 2-liter soda bottles, boil-in-the-bag pouches for frozen foods, and microwave food trays.
No. 2	High-density polyethylene (HDPE)	This denotes stuff like laundry detergent bottles and motor oil bottles, milk jugs, aspirin bottles—that kind of thicker plastic.
No. 3	Polyvinyl chloride (PVC)	This is clear food and nonfood packaging, including cooking oil bottles, medical tubing, wire, cable insulation, etc.
No. 4	Low-density polyethylene (LDPE)	This includes dry-cleaning bags, bread bags, frozen-food bags, the plastic wrap that you use to cover food, the bags you pull off the roll in the grocery store's produce department, and also certain squeezable bottles, like for mustard.
No. 5	Polypropylene (PP)	This kind of plastic is used for certain medicine bottles, tough plastics that resist heat and moisture. It's also used for yogurt containers, shampoo bottles, straws, margarine tubs, and syrup bottles.
No. 6	Polystyrene (PS)	This is actually plastic foam, better known as Styrofoam. It is used for grocery store meat trays, egg cartons, plastic plates, cups used for hot drinks, plastic cutlery, fast-food clamshell containers.
No. 7	Other	Code 7 indicates a plastic made with a resin that's not one of these other six codes, or a plastic made from more than one individual resin.

might have different guidelines (or other facilities). You can find out more from your local municipality or from the community relations people at factories in your area.

Because I couldn't recycle them, I avoided 3 and 5 plastics when possible. I looked at an item before I bought it and if it had a *3* or a *5* on the bottom, I would see if I could get the same product that wasn't packaged in a no. 3 or no. 5 resin. Unfortunately, there're certain things that come in 3 and 5 only and they're products that you need, so you buy them.

There's another reason I tend to avoid no. 3 resin. PVC is one of the *least* environmentally friendly materials around. People have actually gone so far as to call it *evil,* and not without reason. I'll let my friend Josh Bradley from 360 Interchange tell you more about PVC, and about a new material called ecoFoam, which in many cases can replace no. 3 resin.

Ed's Green Friend: ecoFoam

PVC (polyvinyl chloride) is one of the most ubiquitous and most destructive materials made by man. It's also one of the most versatile plastics.

We interact with PVC almost every minute of every day. When you start your day, you're likely having your first contact with PVC, since it can be used in ***mattresses, pillows, pillow covers,*** and ***mattress covers.*** Your contact with this plastic continues as you walk across the ***carpet*** to the bathroom, where you pull back the ***shower curtain*** and water flows through ***PVC piping.*** Then you walk on a ***vinyl floor*** in the kitchen, where you reach into the ***refrigerator*** and pull out food wrapped in ***plastic*** for breakfast. On your way out the door, you stop to pick up some of your ***children's toys,*** then slide onto your car's ***vinyl seat*** and prepare to drive away while enjoying that ***"new car" smell.*** After work, you come home to water your lawn with your ***garden hose*** or your ***sprinklers,*** then relax in the ***plastic patio furniture.***

PVC is all around us because of its versatility, ease of assembly, and low cost, but at what price to our health and environment?

The production of PVC creates vinyl chloride monomer (VCM) and hydrogen chloride (HCl), both of which have been linked to dramatic health issues, including liver cancer, respiratory damage, failure of the circulatory system, and death. Equally dangerous are the plasticizers used to make PVC more flexible for many of the products we use. These additives, called ***phthalates,*** help to create everything from the soft plastic toys that your children play with to the IV bags that provide vital fluids in the hospital. An EPA website lists more than 190 articles on the potential hazards of phthalates. Many places, including Japan and the European Union countries, have banned the use of some phthalates because of their impact on children's health and their tendency to leach into the water system.

Throughout the entire life cycle of products made from PVC, we find damage to health and the environment. PVC is not degradable, it's difficult to recycle, and it releases toxic fumes when burned. That means the 7 billion pounds of waste per year—and the 300 billion pounds of PVC nearing the end of its useful life—have all the makings of an environmental catastrophe.

Seventy percent of this waste comes from homes. We have the power to buy products made from less damaging, more easily recyclable plastics—and from more traditional materials, such as wood, glass, and natural fibers.

Plus, a new material called ecoFoam can replace PVC for most applications, without the harm to our bodies and our environment. Though still a petroleum-based product, ecoFoam uses no heavy metals in production. It contains no chlorine or phthalates. And it does not outgas toxic fumes. Additionally, the material is photodegradable and recyclable, so many generations of products can be made from the same amount of original material.

EcoFoam can take a variety of forms, from a soft foam to a more dense, rubberlike foam, as well as a material that can replace vinyl, making it nearly as versatile as PVC. Also, ecoFoam's lightweight, closed-cell construction makes it resistant to moisture absorption, and it can be formulated to dampen sound and vibration. It also can be combined with other materials to increase strength—even laminated onto fabrics. And in most cases, ecoFoam can replace PVC with little to no effect on manufacturing processes, which makes it a logical next step in removing PVC from our daily lives.

—Josh Bradley

So that's PVC, which is no. 3 plastic. And then there's no. 6 plastic, better known as Styrofoam. I certainly do not buy Styrofoam in any form. But whether you buy it or not, you're going to get some Styrofoam. If someone sends me something with Styrofoam packing material in the box, I am never going to throw it away. I'll reuse it as a packing material or take it to a recycling program.

The plastic industry claims—and I take them at their word—that they want people to recycle Styrofoam, and so they take these things back in cities across the nation. It should be easy to do a Google search and find a place in your area that accepts Styrofoam. So before I could throw it in the blue bin, I would save no. 6 plastic. Rachelle and I even have friends who would bring their Styrofoam to our house. And then I took it to a place in the City of Commerce called Free Flow Packaging two or three times a year.

And there's other stuff that supposedly cannot be recycled, like plastic bags. You can't put them in most cities' recycling bin. But there are dry cleaners and markets that will take plastic bags back. You just have to do a little research and a little legwork.

RECYCLING PAPER

There're all kinds of paper: white office paper, notebook paper, paper napkins, paper towels, milk cartons, newspapers, magazines, catalogs, paper shopping bags, junk mail, toilet paper rolls, telephone books, corrugated cardboard boxes used for shipping, chipped cardboard boxes such as cereal boxes. And most of that paper can be recycled. Most of it is also accepted by cities' curbside recycling programs.

But while I could put pretty much all my waste paper into the blue curbside recycling bin in L.A., for extra credit, I save certain kinds of paper—my white office paper and my colored paper—and I shred it up and use it as packing material when I ship my cleaning products, Begley's Best. And if I've shredded all I can use, I take the rest of that paper to Alpha Recycling in

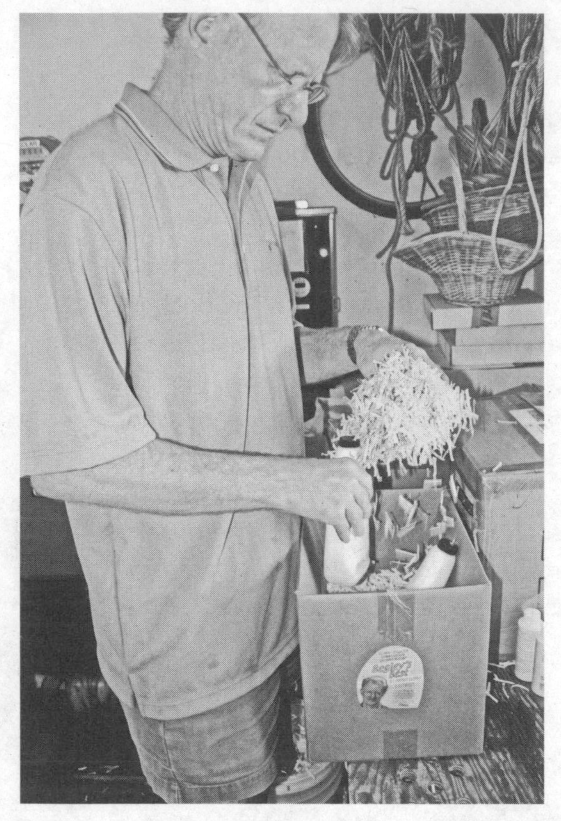

I use shredded waste paper as packing material.

North Hollywood. There, I can put it in the white and colored-paper bins.

Why go the extra step? Because the mixed paper that's going in the blue curbside recycling bin will be used mostly for backing material for roofing tiles. It's a very low grade. Think about it: It gets mixed in with old tuna fish cans, and most people don't rinse things out really well. What kind of paper is it after it's been mixed in with everything else? It's a crappy paper, so it doesn't get a high use.

My good white paper and colored paper that's clean and dry is a higher-quality recyclable. It can even, conceivably, be made into paper again, or into file folders or something like that.

What about recycling newspapers? Newspapers are absolutely recyclable—every part of them, even the glossy inserts—and you can mix brown paper grocery bags in with newspaper, too.

We've been recycling newspaper in this country for decades—for a profit. When newspaper gets recycled, it often gets made into newsprint again, or it gets made into corrugated boxes or folding boxes.

Magazines can also be recycled in curbside bins. Of course, you can find other ways to recycle magazines, too. You can donate them to a library or a veterans hospital or a doctor's office. You can even use the pages as gift

lightbulb for four hours. If every single morning newspaper in the United States were

wrap or let your kids use them for arts and crafts projects. The same goes for catalogs.

Phone books are another easy-to-recycle item. Just put them in your curbside bin, along with most of your junk mail (you just need to pull out any stuff like magnets or product samples first).

You can put corrugated cardboard into curbside recycling bins, too. And if you're recycling boxes or office paper, you don't have to worry about removing staples. They'll get taken care of during the recycling process. But you do need to remove packing tape.

The one exception, with regard to recycling cardboard, is dirty cardboard. Things like greasy pizza boxes can't be recycled. They're just going to contaminate the other stuff you and your neighbors put in your recycling bins, so they have to go in the trash.

Other paper that cannot be recycled includes wax paper, paper that's been contaminated with food, carbon paper, thermal fax paper, paper with a sticky backing (like stickers and Post-its), and paper that's been laminated.

Because they have a waxy coating, milk cartons and juice boxes cannot be recycled. Well, technically, they can be recycled, but the process is so difficult and so expensive that very few companies are recycling that stuff right now. A few cities' curbside recycling programs will take milk cartons, like the program in Boston. But this stuff mainly does not get recycled right now. So when I go to buy milk or juice at the store, I choose to buy it packaged in a glass container—or if I can't, then I'll buy it in a recyclable plastic container.

Hazardous Waste

Hazardous waste comes in so many forms. Hazardous waste is AAA batteries, 12-volt batteries, car batteries. Hazardous waste is hearing-aid batteries. Hazardous waste is old paint cans. Hazardous waste is old household cleaning products. Hazardous waste is e-waste—that is to say, electronic waste—an old computer monitor, an old printer, an old computer.

recycled, we'd save 41,000 trees a day. And we'd avoid sending 6 million tons of waste to

All of this hazardous waste contains toxic elements that wind up in a landfill and leach into the water table or otherwise enter our environment. So at the most basic level, anything toxic or corrosive is considered hazardous. That includes:

- oven cleaners
- drain cleaners
- wood polish
- metal polish
- toilet bowl cleaners
- tub, tile, and shower cleaners
- bleach
- pool chemicals
- motor oil, transmission fluid, and brake fluid
- carburetor and fuel injection system cleaners
- antifreeze
- air-conditioning refrigerant
- rat poison
- flea repellents
- mothballs
- bug sprays
- roach traps
- snail pellets
- weed killers
- adhesives and glues
- oil- or enamel-based paint
- wood stains
- paint thinners and turpentine
- paint strippers and removers
- photographic chemicals
- driveway sealer
- batteries
- mercury thermostats or thermometers
- fluorescent lightbulbs, which contain mercury
- incandescent lightbulbs, which contain lead

Dispose of Hazardous Waste Responsibly
COST: free or nearly free

landfills. **Each year, Americans generate 1.6 million tons of household hazardous waste.**

Flammable products, anything that can be ignited, are also considered hazardous waste. Things including:

- propane tanks and other compressed gas cylinders
- kerosene
- home heating oil
- diesel fuel
- gasoline and oil mixed together
- lighter fluid
- automotive starter fluid

Sadly, most people don't realize that a fraction of these things are hazardous waste. And they also don't realize that disposing of such products in their trash cans will reintroduce them one day to their environment, their children's environment.

People usually have a lot of this stuff lying around. An average home can accumulate as much as 100 pounds of this hazardous waste—in the basement, in the garage, in sheds, and in closets.

So how do you dispose of hazardous waste? Responsibly, I hope. Many cities have a designated hazardous waste pickup day. It's also quite easy to find drop-off locations. People regularly write me after watching the show *Living with Ed:* "I heard you talk about disposing of hazardous waste. I'm in Texas and we don't have anything like that here. Where do you dispose in a place like Texas?" And I Google "hazardous waste pickup Texas." Turns out there's a place in Austin. So I e-mail them back, "You said you lived near Austin. There's one in Austin. There's one in Houston." All you have to do is do a Google search for "hazardous waste" and your city, and you will find one in your area. "Hazardous waste Albany." "Hazardous waste Schenectady." You're going to find a hazardous waste pickup or drop-off service in your city or very near your city.

I never throw away any of that stuff. I certainly don't buy any nonrechargeable batteries. Occasionally we'll get something that has them, and I use them until they run out. So I get a few without even purchasing them, and those have to be recycled maybe once a year. If one of the many compact fluorescent bulbs I have goes out, if it's finally seen the end of its fifteen-

According to the EPA, 50 percent of all paper, 34 percent of all plastic soft drink bottles, 45

to seventeen-year life, it has to be dealt with. I have a shoe box in the garage, and it takes me a year or so to fill it with batteries and things like that.

There are other options for dealing with hazardous waste, too, specialty programs. Let's say you've got some leftover paint. You certainly don't want to throw partially full paint cans in the trash. Regular oil-based paint and latex paint are hazardous waste. And even if you were using nontoxic, biodegradable paint, there're better things to do with the leftovers than to send them to a landfill. Many cities have what's called a *paint exchange.* You bring in your leftover paint. It gets sorted right there on the spot. And then people who need paint can get those leftovers for free, right then and there. Some cities also collect leftover paint and use it for their beautification efforts or to paint over graffiti. So you can find environmentally sound ways to get rid of almost anything.

COMPUTER AND ELECTRONICS RECYCLING

Household electronics items—like televisions, printers, fax machines, computer monitors, keyboards, computer mice, VCRs, cell phones—all these things are hazardous waste. In many cases, they can contain stuff like lead, mercury, cadmium, and chromium. Stuff you definitely don't want leaching into your groundwater.

I know there's a lot of pressure to upgrade this stuff. But I try to use a piece of electronic hardware as long as it's functioning and current enough to just work. I stuck with Windows 98 for a long time—until it just didn't work for what I needed to do. I had to upgrade to XP, and I had to get a new computer. But I try to stick with the technologies for as long as I can. And then I usually give my computer, which is still working well, since I take care of it myself, to a family member—a grown son or daughter, my young daughter—and recycle that way.

percent of all aluminum beer and soft drink cans, 63 percent of all steel packaging, and 67

But when something finally craps out—a cell phone, a printer, a computer that can't be fixed—that's considered e-waste, electronic waste. And there are places that will take it.

There's a very good e-waste bill that passed in California, which was the first state to adopt this sort of approach. There's a premium, a deposit, that you pay for every monitor, every printer that you buy in California. It's a small sum, like $5 for a monitor. And that deposit pays for the program. Basically, that stuff is taken back and the mercury is taken out, the lead is taken out, and then it's recycled.

These old electronics items used to be shipped over to Asia to be refurbished and resold. But now it's more cost effective to fully recycle the e-waste here in California.

Now I take my e-waste to SoCal Computer Recyclers in Harbor City. They have a big recycling facility, where I can drop off my e-waste. Also, they've got a lot of corporate accounts, so when some big company decides to replace thousands of PCs, all that e-waste can be recycled. Even companies outside California are having their e-waste shipped to this company to make sure everything gets recycled properly. SoCal also holds events at schools and parks, places throughout the community, so people can drop off e-waste close to home. And they don't just recycle this e-waste. They also make sure to remove any proprietary data—on a computer's hard drive or on a cell phone or on a BlackBerry or what have you. They make sure your data is safely and properly destroyed.

So the bottom line is, if it runs on batteries or gets plugged into the wall, they can recycle it in a way that's good for the environment and good for your privacy, good for things like preventing identity theft.

Reusing: The Easiest Form of Recycling

You know, recycling doesn't always have to mean taking stuff apart and melting it down. *Reusing* things is the easiest form of recycling. I like to give stuff away to Goodwill, and Rachelle likes to sell stuff at a garage sale. She likes the cash.

There's another kind of curbside recycling that a lot of people do every day, and it's great. They put stuff they don't want anymore out on the curb

percent of all major appliances are now recycled. **The idea is to recycle things in a way that**

with a sign that says FREE. It's like Recycling 101. Let someone else, instead of a landfill, have it.

That is what we did with Hayden's old plastic playhouse that she had outgrown. There was no way I was going to send it to a landfill. Somebody with little kids would love to have it. Especially for free.

Donating stuff to a charity is another great way to make sure it gets reused, and you get a tax deduction at the same time. All kinds of charities operate thrift shops—stores where they sell the stuff you donate—and then they use that money to benefit the charity's cause. You can donate stuff to thrift shops that benefit the American Cancer Society, Habitat for Humanity, a local hospital, a homeless shelter, a church, a no-kill pet shelter. Groups like the Salvation Army and Goodwill also have thrift shops, plus they have training and rehabilitation programs, so they may take stuff like an old lamp that needs rewiring or a couch that needs reupholstering.

There are other options, too, besides donating stuff to a charity or leaving it out on the curb or having a garage sale. Freecycle, for example, is a worldwide nonprofit that connects people who want to give stuff away with people who want to get stuff for free. You go on the freecycle.org website and find a group in your area. Then you just post something, and it goes out to this list. You just go, "I've got an old TV stand that's gotten ratty, but it still works. It just needs a new paint job." Someone will probably come and pick that up and be very happy to have it. They have the time to paint it or whatever. If you've got an old lawn mower that's broken or an old TV that doesn't work anymore, you know there's someone out there who knows how to fix it and then can use it or sell it. There's a place for just about anything through freecycle.org.

RACHELLE'S TURN

You can find other ways to help people with your old stuff, too, like prescription glasses. Charities collect them and then they distribute them to people in need, here in the United States and all over the world. You just drop off your old glasses at a store like LensCrafters or Sunglass Hut or a Pearle

they'll actually get used at the highest level possible, so you can save the most natural resources

Vision center. The store collects them and then gives them to a charity like Give the Gift of Sight.

You can do the same kind of thing with an old cell phone. It's kind of ironic, but it's actually cheaper to provide cell service than it is to build all the infrastructure for old-fashioned landline telephones in some underdeveloped countries. So if you donate an old cell phone that's just junk to you—it's just cluttering up your closet—you literally can provide a lifeline for someone in another country.

Buy Recycled

Buy Recycled Products
COST: minimal

Now, everything we've discussed so far is really important. But it's not enough just to recycle or to find someone who can reuse your old stuff. Unless you're *buying* recycled products, you're not really recycling.

Why? Because recycling programs only work when there's a *demand* for recycled products. If people don't buy recycled products, companies won't make them. Then things that *can* be recycled wind up going unused. They wind up in a landfill simply because there's no need for them.

So buy every envelope, every sheet of paper, everything you can that's recycled. The products are out there. You just have to go online to a search engine and type "recycled envelopes," "recycled paper," "recycled fences," "recycled lawn furniture." Buy it. It's out there.

All the paper that I use in my printer—and in every way—is 100 percent postconsumer recycled paper. That's great.

And that's an important point: *Recycled paper* can mean different things. It can be called 100 percent recycled paper and still be from the paper mill. It's just the end of the roll and the stuff they chop off. So yes, it's recycled, but it's just what's left over when they make paper. They didn't have 8 by 11-inch pieces, so they put those scraps in their recycling bin.

And that's fine; it's still reusing their waste. It's not a bad thing. But it's

and the most energy. Americans buy more than 85 million tons of paper per year. That's

not as good as *postconsumer* recycled paper. That's made from the stuff you and I and businesses all across the country have put into recycling bins.

One hundred percent postconsumer recycled paper is now available—and it has been for some time—even with the Staples logo on it. It used to be that you had to buy some off brand, some earth-friendly paper, and maybe it was 50 percent postconsumer waste, and it was a lot of money per ream. They didn't make much of it. But now they've got it down, making recycled paper, and they're doing it in an environmentally sound way.

And we're not just talking about paper for your printer or copy machine. We're talking about all different kinds of recycled paper.

According to the Natural Resources Defense Council:

- If every household in the U.S. bought just one box of 100 percent recycled tissue (175 sheets) instead of one box of virgin-fiber facial tissue, we could save 163,000 trees.
- If every household bought just one roll of 100 percent recycled toilet paper (500 sheets) instead of one roll of virgin-fiber toilet paper, we could save another 423,900 trees.
- If every household bought just one roll of 100 percent recycled paper towels (70 sheets) instead of virgin-fiber, we could save another 544,000 trees.
- And if every household bought just one package of 100 percent recycled paper napkins (250 count) instead of virgin-fiber, we could save another one million trees.

Suffice to say those little choices at the grocery store really add up to a huge difference when we're talking about natural resources being saved.

So what else can you buy that's recycled? All kinds of things.

I line the trash can in my kitchen with Seventh Generation recycled plastic trash bags. I've done it the other way. I've had a trash can with no bag. But then, living in L.A., where water comes at such an environmental cost,

about 700 pounds per person. Save your old laser printer cartridges. They can be recycled,

you're having to regularly use a lot of water and soap and effort to clean out a trash can. You really need to have some sort of a bag, so I buy these recycled Seventh Generation bags and put my trash in them.

You know, for many years, the problem with plastic was that it would never break down. You'd put it in a landfill and it would be there forever, intact. Well, now companies are making things from recycled plastic that you don't *want* to break down. So that's no longer a problem. Now that's an asset. A good example is our white picket fence made from recycled milk jugs. That's a good thing for the environment, to get those milk jugs out of the waste stream. But also, this fence never needs to be painted. It never has any bug, like termites, that attacks it. Water never damages it. It's like a hundred-year fence. So where the problem with plastic was that it never breaks down, now the good thing about plastic is that it never breaks down.

The same goes for a deck or an outdoor staircase that's made from 100 percent postconsumer recycled plastic lumber. It never has to be painted. It never has to be stained. And it never breaks down.

So buying recycled isn't just good for the environment, it's good for your lifestyle. You don't have to waste time or money stripping your picket fence or your deck and refinishing it every couple of years.

Natural and Recycled Furniture

You can also find different kinds of recycled furniture. First off, there's used furniture. When you buy a piece that already exists, you cut down on the amount of furniture being made, which cuts down on energy use. It cuts down on trees being felled and then turned into lumber. It cuts down on the energy used to truck that lumber to a manufacturing facility. And it cuts down on the energy used to truck that finished furniture to a warehouse and then to a store. Who knew antiquing could be so good for the earth, right?

RACHELLE'S TURN

When I decorate my home, I try to make it personal and not look like it came straight out of a furniture catalog. It doesn't take a lot of money to add your own personal touches. In fact, I like shopping at flea markets to find unique items. And I'm recycling at the same time.

refilled, or rebuilt—stores like Staples will even give you a few dollars' credit for bringing in

There's another environmentally sound option, too. You can purchase new furniture that's made from recycled materials. Manufacturers have found ways to take used wood, used metal, and other used materials and transform them into completely new pieces. There're even companies making outdoor garden furniture from recycled plastic lumber.

If you do decide to buy brand-new furniture—stuff that's not recycled—at least make sure it's made from natural products, like wood. By cutting down on the use of plastic and other new synthetic materials, you save oil and other fuels.

And speaking of wood, look for furniture made from *sustainable* wood. Rather than using old-fashioned clear-cutting techniques that decimate forests and wildlife, companies that offer sustainable-wood products maintain the health and productivity of forests and their ecosystems. You can find furniture made from sustainable wood at very mainstream retailers, like Ikea. And if you want to build your own furniture, you can find wood certified by the Forest Stewardship Council in stores like Lowe's and Home Depot.

Recycled Countertops

RACHELLE'S TURN

I've been wanting to redo the kitchen in our little house for a long time. So I started small. I found a company that makes countertops out of recycled glass. I thought Ed would like that. But first he was more concerned with what would happen to the ugly old tile that was already on our countertops. With Ed, it's all about where's it going. It's really not the money he's worried about. The reason we never upgrade around here is because he's all concerned about creating waste.

Fortunately, we discovered that we were having a positive effect on the environment. We were keeping far more glass out of a landfill than the waste we were creating with that ugly old tile. And who

your empties. The caps for most plastic containers are not made from the same type of

knows, the company that installed our counters may even have a way to recycle the old materials they remove. Wouldn't that be great?

This stuff we used for our new countertops is called Vetrazzo, and it's made from many different things. Recycled Coke bottles, recycled traffic-light lenses, recycled glass of every form. They use different materials to come up with different colors and designs. I think it's a creative way to take objects that most would consider trash and turn them into something functional and beautiful. Vetrazzo's material is very visually appealing, and it's recycled, so it's good on many counts.

The countertop that Rachelle and I ended up choosing is called Hollywood Sage, and it's made from broken-up soda bottles. Over a thousand bottles were used just to make the countertop for our small kitchen. So we actually wound up taking a lot of glass out of the waste stream. And I feel good about that.

Precycling

There's *recycling,* which is very important. And then there's *precycling,* which is every bit as important. When I'm shopping, if there's one package for razor blades that's a foot long for a little tiny thing of blades, and there's another package that's smaller, I'm always going to buy the smaller one. At certain stores, you can buy five containers of razor blades in one package. Whatever you can do to reduce the amount of packaging you buy—by buying in bulk, by buying things in the smallest amount of packaging possible—is really huge.

And when they say, "Paper or plastic?" at the grocery store checkout line, the answer is always "Neither." Pull out your canvas bag or string bag. If you don't have either, reuse your old paper or plastic bags. Most places that I shop at give you a nickel per bag credit for bringing your bags back—canvas, plastic, or paper—giving us a financial incentive to recycle.

plastic as the containers themselves, so you should remove the caps before recycling the

So buy things with the least amount of packaging, and don't take any new paper or plastic bags. I keep canvas bags in the trunk of my car so that I have them whenever I decide to stop at the store.

Naysayers will say it takes energy to make these canvas bags, too, but I've got canvas bags from the '80s. These bags last a long time.

Sometimes you just have to choose paper or plastic. Now that I have a business, Begley's Best, some people just insist on getting a plastic bag so they can buy a product and then carry the bottle around the city market where I sell it. Most people, however, bring their own plastic bags when they come and buy my stuff. They know me enough to do that. Forget about knowing me—they just do it because they know it's a good idea. But when people want me to give them a plastic bag to carry one, two, sometimes three plastic bottles at a farmers' market, I have thousands of them. I have friends save bags for me. The bags have to be clean. They can't have crushed tomatoes at the bottom of them, obviously. I save those bags and then I reuse them.

Here's another great way you can precycle. We buy kitty litter in bulk, and then we just keep bringing back the same big pail and refilling it. It's a huge pail, and it's got two different UPC codes on it. There's one that the cashier scans the first time you buy the pail, and then there's another code to scan for a refill. So I just keep bringing back this same pail—it's a five-year-old pail at this point, easily—and that way I don't buy any new packaging for kitty litter. I have two of these pails, so when one is empty, I'll put it out by the car so I know to bring it into Petco. And I just go to the big bin there with the scooper and fill it up again.

RACHELLE'S TURN

Here's another good one. I've heard that plastic water bottles are really bad for you. We put them in our cars, and then they heat up and the plastic gets into our water. That can't be good for us. And then there are just all these little water bottles everywhere, and they don't break down.

containers. Never dump hazardous waste—or any trash—into your city's storm drains. What

But there's a new water bottle, available from New Wave Enviro (newwaveenviro.com). It's made of corn. It's biodegradable, so it will break down in nature. And it has this filter. It costs $10—it's a pricey little water bottle. However, you can refill it and it can filter tap water. You just have to wash it, and you have ninety fills. Ninety!

Look how much packaging you save just by buying this one water bottle—and it's keeping toxic chemicals out of your body at the same time.

Saving paper also fits into this category called precycling. To save paper, I pay bills online. Companies are making it easier for you, too. They don't want to get a piece of paper in the mail and pay a person to open it. It's so much easier to have one person point and click than six people with letter openers doing all that work.

They have online bill-pay programs that you can certainly do through your bank nowadays. Moreover, you don't even have to point and click. It's just taken out automatically—your mortgage payment every month, your cell phone, gas, you name it. You can approve them—for example, Cingular Wireless or Time Warner Cable—and they post it; others show you, like "Here's your bill, so you make sure we're not going to charge you $1,200 by accident. It's the same as it was last month, some $124 for a premium package. And here's your cellular bill for your wife's phone and yours. If you don't like it, click here. And if you do like it, you do nothing." They just take it out of your account. There's more and more of that, and it's easy to do.

Also, I do as much as I can by e-mail. Most people do that today. I try to generate as little paper as possible.

Another great thing you can do: If you pack a sack lunch, don't use plastic sandwich bags. Pack things in glass or plastic containers. Then you can reuse your own containers over and over and over again.

Rechargeable Batteries

Another way you can reduce waste is by choosing rechargeable batteries instead of disposables. I've been using rechargeable batteries since 1978, and

goes into most of these drains flows untreated into rivers, lakes, or oceans. Check to see if

I'm glad they're good for the environment. That's the reason I did it. But what I quickly learned is that they're really good for my pocketbook. I wasn't buying as many Duracells, as many Energizers, as many Rayovacs. I just wasn't buying as many batteries.

Back in those days, the rechargeable batteries were nickel-cadmium. Cadmium, of course, is an element that has to be disposed of properly. I never once threw one in the trash. I would save them and take them to the hazardous waste disposal site.

I must say, those old rechargeable batteries would conk out on you much quicker than today's batteries. Today's batteries, as we know, are much more advanced. They're nickel-metal hydride, they're lithium-ion batteries. They work much better.

Why? Because, sadly, those old nickel-cadmium batteries were like people. They remembered how you treated them. If you didn't fully charge or discharge them, they didn't like that, and they never got a full charge again. So nobody's buying nickel-cadmium for anything anymore.

The standard has long since changed to nickel-metal hydride, and now you can get even more watts per kilogram from lithium-ion and others, like lithium-titanate batteries, which are wonderful.

I'm working with a company called Altairnano, which has these wonderful lithium-titanate batteries that don't have the challenges that other lithium-ion batteries have. They don't heat up. They just don't have those safety and other problems. Those are the batteries in my Phoenix Motorcars electric truck, and I'm hoping they'll become available for other applications soon.

Rechargeable batteries in general are just much better than nonrechargeable ones because *all* batteries are toxic. But rechargeable batteries last longer. They're better for the environment in that way, and they put money in your pocket.

People say, "Oh, these rechargeable batteries, they're toxic!"

What is a Duracell? An Energizer? A Rayovac? These have toxic elements, too. You can't throw those in the trash. But people feel very free to throw those little Coppertops away. You *can't* throw them away. They're toxic. You're supposed to dispose of them properly. And see how quickly you fill up a shoe box with batteries if you're not buying rechargeable.

Beyond that, you have options that require no batteries at all. As we've

your city has a special program after the holidays to recycle Christmas trees into mulch,

known for many, many years, you can store power in a capacitor. I have these flashlights that I sell on my website. You shake them up. It's the Faraday principle: A magnet passes through the coil, and electrons are generated. But where are those electrons stored? In a battery? No, not in this device. They're stored in a capacitor. And so you turn on the light—which is not a lightbulb; it's an LED, a light-emitting diode—and you have wonderful light whenever you need it. And it's stored not in a battery, which will wear out over time, but in a capacitor, which has a far, far longer life expectancy. So it's a much better choice for something you'd need in an emergency—like a flashlight—and for so many other reasons. It's another very good way to go.

So Many Ways to Recycle

So now we've come up with dozens—if not hundreds—of things that you can recycle. Glass jars and their lids. Cardboard boxes. Laundry detergent bottles. Eyeglasses. Newspapers. Aluminum cans. Toys. Even a tattered old throw rug. And we've come up with dozens more recycled products that you can buy. Things you'd buy anyway, without even having to choose recycled products—things like cans of soda and bottles of juice, like a newspaper. And then there are all those things you can specifically seek out that are made using postconsumer waste, such as recycled office paper and file folders and toilet paper and outdoor furniture.

All of these recycling efforts provide benefits on so many levels. They reduce the amount of stuff going into landfills. They reduce the need to use up new natural resources. And they reduce the amount of *energy* spent mining those resources—often in distant locales—and the amount of energy spent transporting those resources to the United States to be made into whatever it is we think we need.

So now let's take a look at energy from a different angle. Let's look at ways to create energy in an environmentally friendly manner, as well as ways to reduce your need for energy from outside sources.

which is then given or sold to people for use in their gardens.

ENERGY

SUN, WIND, COAL, WATER—WHERE DOES YOUR ELECTRICITY COME FROM?

4

Most people get the electricity for their home—or their business—from their local utility company. They pay the going rate, and they use what they need. They may take steps to reduce their energy use, like implementing some of the techniques I covered in Chapter 1, "Home." But people typically don't even know they have a choice when it comes to *how* their electricity is produced and *by whom*.

Well, I'm here to tell you: You *do* have a choice. Actually, you have a lot of choices. You can produce your own electricity, as I do using solar panels and a wind turbine mounted on the roof of my home. You can even sell some of the excess electricity you produce back to your local utility company.

But what if you don't own your home? What if you're on a tight budget? Or what if you live in a restrictive community that has rules against things like solar panels on your roof? Well, there are other options. For instance, you can still buy electricity from your local utility company, but you can choose to participate in a green power program. And if your local electric company doesn't have such a program, you may be able to switch to another provider that does.

And even beyond all that—whether you do all of the above or none of the above—you can take steps to offset any carbon dioxide emissions produced by the electricity you do use.

And that brings us to the heart of the matter. Every source of electricity has consequences; it affects the environment. It's just that some sources of electricity are more environmentally friendly—actually a lot more environmentally friendly—than others.

How Electricity Is Produced

Let's start by looking at all the different ways electricity is produced. The most common is by burning things to create heat, which in turn creates steam. That steam is then used to turn a big turbine, and that generates electricity.

A lot of different materials are burned to create electricity, including

- coal (still the primary way utility companies create power in the United States)
- crude oil
- natural gas
- garbage
- biomass (which is typically waste from the manufacturing of paper and pulp products)
- methane—the gas that's emitted from landfills

There are also ways to produce electricity using steam that don't involve burning things. For instance, you can create nuclear reactions, or you can use the heat from the earth to create *geothermal* power.

Solar is clearly a renewable source of energy. So is wind. So is geothermal power. And so is

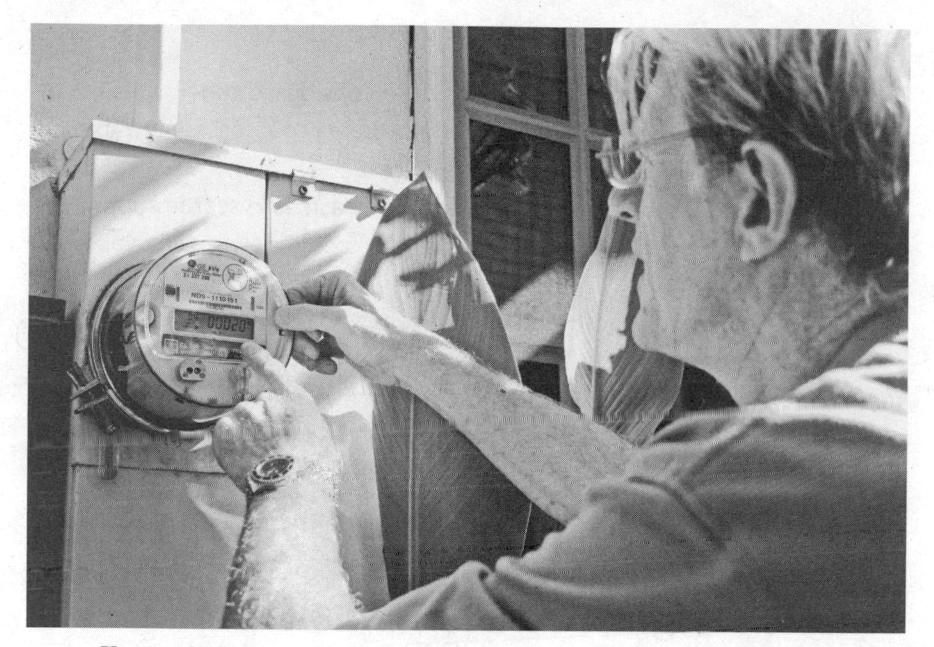

How much electricity does your home use? I use 1,200 kilowatt-hours a month.

There are also steam-free ways to generate electricity, among them:

- Hydroelectric power. In this case, the force of falling or flowing water turns a turbine.
- Wind power. You can literally harness the wind to create power using windmills—or, more precisely, wind turbines.
- Solar power. The energy of the sun can also be harnessed to create power. Big solar electric power plants either use the heat of the sun to produce steam, which then turns a turbine or some other kind of generator, or they use photovoltaic (PV) cells to convert solar energy directly into electricity.

So these are the primary ways utility companies all across the United States create the electricity that powers your home and your workplace and your city.

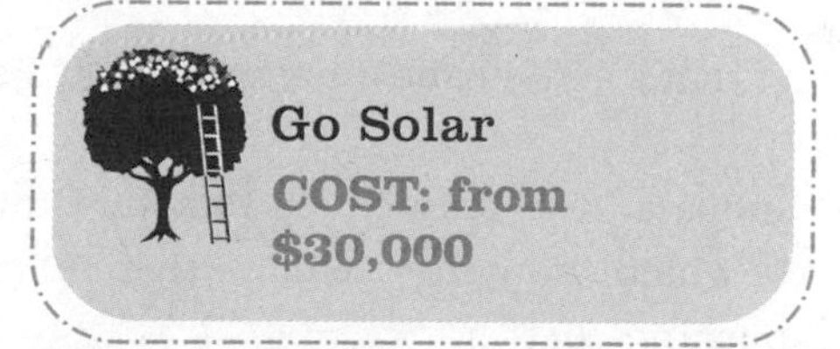

power generated by burning biomass or by burning methane gas at a landfill or by burning

Renewable vs. Green

Now, some of these sources of electricity are considered *renewable*, meaning they don't require the use of limited natural resources. Renewable resources are generally considered inexhaustible.

Certainly no one would argue that waste, or trash, is in scarce supply. We obviously make plenty of it in this country. It's definitely a renewable resource.

But, just as certainly, you can see that *renewable energy* is not the same as *green energy*. Yes, waste is considered renewable, but burning waste is certainly not an environmentally friendly way to make power. You're just taking all that often very toxic material and releasing it into the atmosphere. I'm highly opposed to incinerators as a means either of dealing with trash or making power.

Different Region, Different Choices

The mix as to which power sources are used to generate electricity varies from region to region. Here's how it breaks down where I live. The Los Angeles Department of Water and Power (LADWP) generates 47 percent of its power from coal, 29 percent from natural gas, 9 percent from nuclear, 7 percent from large hydroelectric power plants, and 8 percent from renewable power.

On average, the entire state of California produces

- 41.5 percent of its power from natural gas
- 19.0 percent from hydro
- 15.7 percent of its power from coal
- 12.9 percent from nuclear
- 10.9 percent from renewable resources

That's in dramatic contrast to states such as

- Indiana, Kentucky, North Dakota, Utah, West Virginia, and Wyoming, all of which still generate more than 90 percent of their electricity by burning coal

waste. **According to the EPA, the process of generating electricity is the single largest source**

- The District of Columbia, which generates 100 percent of its electricity by burning crude oil
- Rhode Island, which generates 98.9 percent of its electricity by burning natural gas

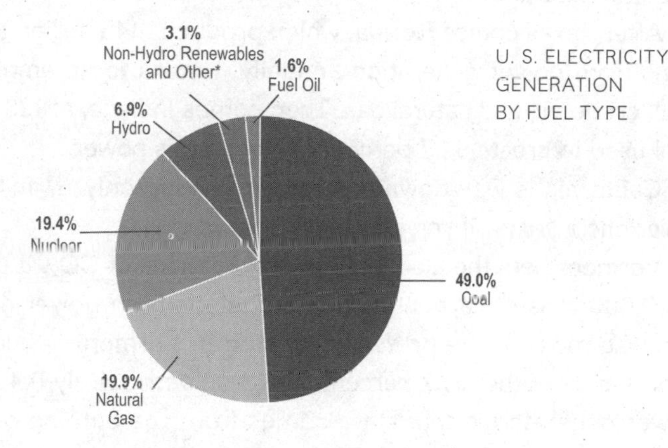

Creating Carbon Dioxide

In most cases, when you generate power at a power plant, you put out carbon dioxide, or CO_2. These emissions come out of the power plant's smokestacks as a result of the combustion process—from burning coal or crude oil or natural gas. Power plants also produce sulfur dioxide, oxides of nitrogen, and mercury emissions, but carbon dioxide is the thing people focus on most because it's considered a primary cause of global warming.

Obviously, the *way* your utility company generates power has a profound effect on how much CO_2 it emits. According to the EPA, for each megawatt-hour of electricity that a utility company produces, it creates

- 2,988 pounds of CO_2 by burning municipal solid waste
- 2,249 pounds of CO_2 by burning coal
- 1,672 pounds of CO_2 by burning oil
- 1,135 pounds of CO_2 by burning natural gas
- 0 pounds of CO_2 by using water to create hydroelectric power
- 0 pounds of CO_2 by using wind
- 0 pounds of CO_2 by using solar power
- 0 pounds of CO_2 by using nuclear power

of CO_2 emissions in the United States. It's responsible for 38 percent of all man-made CO_2

On a state-by-state level, Texas leads the way in CO_2 emissions from power generation, putting out more than 280 million *tons* of carbon dioxide each year. It's no surprise that Texas generates most of its power by burning coal and natural gas.

After Texas comes Florida, which produces 145 million tons of CO_2 emissions from power generation annually, thanks to an emphasis on burning coal, crude oil, and natural gas. Then comes Indiana, at 133 million tons, with coal used to create 94.7 percent of the state's power.

California is way down the list, producing only 67 million tons of CO_2 emissions a year—if you can use the word *only*.

Vermont gets the cleanest ranking in terms of CO_2. It produces just shy of 19,000 tons of carbon dioxide emissions from power generation. That's because most of the power generated in Vermont is nuclear—70.5 percent—and another 21.7 percent is hydroelectric. Only 0.4 percent of all the power generated in that state comes from the burning of fossil fuels, and then we're talking oil and gas—not coal. So it's a really clean state in terms of CO_2 emissions, though nuclear power certainly has its drawbacks, which we'll get into later.

The Grid

Now, how does electricity get from a power plant to your home or workplace? The utility company sends that electricity out over a network of transmission and distribution lines, better known as *the grid.*

Transmission lines are those large, high-voltage power lines you see, usually supported by tall metal towers. They move electricity from the power plant to a local substation.

From the substation—or from a transformer—the power then travels over smaller, lower-voltage *distribution lines.* These are the power lines you see overhead along city streets, supported by what we usually think of as *telephone* poles. If you don't see those lines overhead, your city probably has its distribution lines underground.

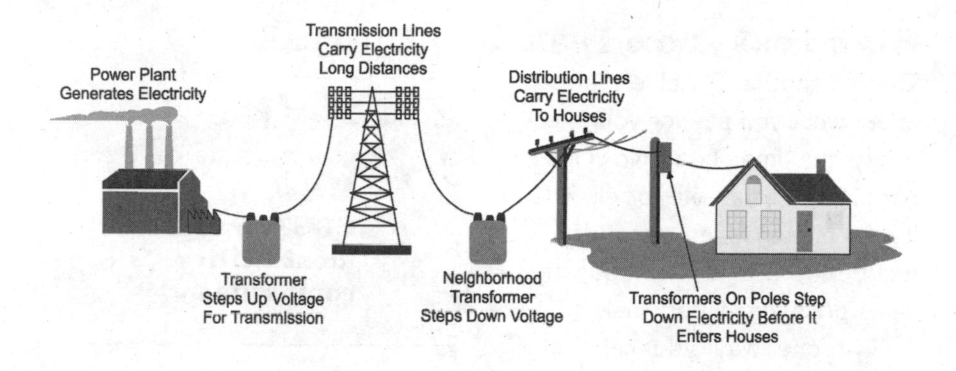

The Price of Electricity

Once you get your electricity, of course you have to pay for it. For home use, electricity is measured in kilowatt-hours. Your electric meter tracks the number of kilowatt-hours you use, then the utility company charges you a price per kilowatt-hour.

We've seen a rapid rise in the price of electricity over the last few years. The curve has started to go up and up and up, and now we're starting to see a real spike. And over time, I think the price of electricity is only going to continue going up.

The price you'll actually pay for electricity varies pretty dramatically by state and by city. In a place like Los Angeles, the LADWP charges 7¢ a kilowatt-hour. Overall, the rate for California averages 12.36¢ per kilowatt-hour.

Hawaii has the highest rate in the nation, averaging 19.05¢ per kilowatt-hour. Electricity is very expensive there because you have to bring in a lot of the fuel from off the islands.

If you go to a place like Idaho, where they've got hydroelectric plants from the 1930s that have well since been paid off, they're charging an average of 4.75¢ a kilowatt-hour. It's the cheapest in the country.

Capital investments to build new power plants impact electricity prices, too. And prices can also fluctuate on a seasonal basis, going up in the summertime, for instance, when demand and usage are much higher.

whatever type of fuel it uses—has a lot to do with the price you pay for electricity. By

High Peak, Low Peak, and Off-Peak

There's another variable that can affect what you pay for your electricity: the time of day. Now, most people pay a flat rate for electricity, no matter what time of day or night they use it. They pay the same price, no matter what.

But one way you can save some money on your electric bill, *if* you can control when you use power, is by doing what I did: I had a time-of-use meter installed at my house. Most electric meters just keep track of how many kilowatt-hours you use. A time-of-use meter keeps track of *when* you use that power, too.

It has three tiers for electricity:

HIGH PEAK. Peak power is very expensive. That's power that is used from 1 P.M. to 5 P.M., when the drain on the grid is heaviest. That's when you may experience brownouts and when power stations tend to go down. People have the air conditioner on. Everybody's in their office with their laser printer on. People are at home watching soap operas on their plasma TVs.

Any power company will tell you that one to five is the period of highest activity, so they charge you the most for power during peak hours if you have a time-of-use meter. Peak power hours are when utility companies have to buy more power for the grid. They buy power from Canada. They buy it from Utah. They buy and sell it on an exchange. And it costs them more when they have to buy this extra power, so they charge you more. High peak is very expensive. That's like 14¢ a kilowatt-hour if you use power then, according to the LADWP.

LOW PEAK. This is from 10 A.M. to 1 P.M. and 5 P.M. to 8 P.M. During these two time slots, the price is just a little more than what you would normally pay if you were to buy your power at a flat rate, regardless of the time of day.

OFF-PEAK. All other hours outside of high peak and low peak are considered off-peak—that is, from 8 P.M. to 10 A.M., as well as weekends. I men-

buying most of your power off-peak, clearly you can save a lot on your electricity bill. If it's

tioned in Chapter 2 that power plants are generating so much extra power that it's wasted. Power plants are surprisingly inefficient structures. They can't just be shut down when the power isn't needed; instead, these huge electric plants are literally doing make-work to shed extra power at night. They're doing things like pumping water uphill so they can use up those extra electrons they don't need. So power companies charge much less for power off-peak because it encourages you to use power when they actually need to get rid of it.

And guess what. I buy nearly all my power from the LADWP off-peak. It starts at less than 4¢ a kilowatt-hour. If I used the exact same amount of energy, but during peak hours, my utility bill would be more than double.

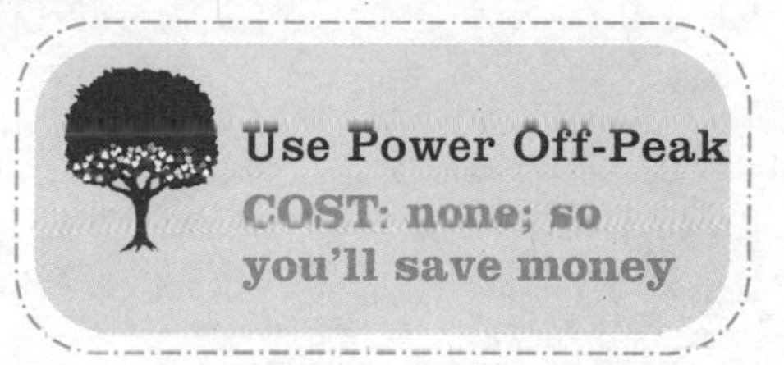

You can do a lot of things off-peak. That's when I do laundry and charge my electric car. You certainly can wait to run the dishwasher until after 8 P.M., or you can run it before you leave for work first thing in the morning. If you're going to be doing a lot of baking or printing out a whole bunch of stuff on your home computer, you also can control when you use that power.

Creating My Own Power

Now, one of the reasons I'm able to buy nearly all my power off-peak from the utility company is because I actually *generate* most of my own electricity—and this is something you may be able to do, too.

Most people don't know this, but I'm a strong supporter of nuclear power. After all, we have the perfect reactor sited in a safe position 93 million miles away cranking out clean power 365 days a year. It's called solar energy. And I know that solar works because it's been running my house and charging my electric car since 1990.

Going solar is something I've been intrigued by since I was a young child. Being the nerd that I was, I pored over the *Edmund Scientific Catalog* and the *Heathkit Catalog,* and I would drool over those solar panels. They were insanely small—and insanely expensive—but I coveted them.

cloudy 180 to 200 days out of the year in your area, don't put up solar; it's not worth it

I clean my solar panels about four times a year, and I see a real current increase.

I believe that solar is the cleanest form of energy. There are no emissions from the panels themselves, and the only emissions involved in the entire process of making solar energy are the minor ones from the manufacture of the panels and from transporting them to the installer and finally to your house.

I was able to take my entire home solar electric in 1990. I've upgraded the system twice, installing fixed arrays of photovoltaic solar panels on the roof of my house and garage, as well as a tracker that follows the sun all day long. The system performs flawlessly.

Now, there's periodic maintenance with anything—well, nearly anything—that you have in your life, and solar panels are no exception. You just need a little bit of water to loosen up the smog dust and the dirt that gets up there. You want to get these panels hosed off, then brushed. So then you see the voltage go up and the current increase—sometimes 20 percent, depending on how much smog dust was on the panels.

economically. But for the rest of the country—nearly all of the country—solar panels make

RACHELLE'S TURN

Ed is so in love with those solar panels. I swear, he spends more time up there on the roof. Really, sometimes I wonder if he's trying to get away from me. He knows I'm afraid of heights, so what does he do? He goes and hides up there on the roof. The neighbors might not like him looking in their windows, though.

I do worry about him, especially when he gets up there to clean the panels four times a year. He's up there with a broom and a hose, washing off all the gunk from the air in L.A. He says it makes the panels work better, and I'm sure it does. But growing up, I never thought the electricity in my house would depend on a man on the roof with a broom.

Stand-Alone vs. Net Metering

My solar electric system was installed in 1990, long before they had *net metering.* So mine is a *stand-alone* system—the kind that is more common in rural areas where there's no electricity available at all.

In other words, I've got between 6 and 7 kilowatts of solar up on the roof—that's a lot—and then I have a big battery storage system in my garage. Thanks to those batteries, I have 2,400 amp-hours of power available at 120 volts. That is a lot of power. It could be cloudy and rainy for a month, and I would still have power for the bare necessities, like my electric teakettle, my computer, a few lights, and the refrigerator. Even on a cloudy or rainy day, though, there is still current going into the system. I have been out in the garage during a heavy rain and witnessed firsthand 5 amps of power going into the system at 120 volts. That is 600 watts of power. So you're still getting something even during the worst weather. You're still going to be able to limp along even if you don't have bright sunshine every day.

And besides, where does it rain for a month? Even in Seattle, it doesn't rain a month straight. So

economic sense. Without subsidies, it can take nearly twenty years to amortize the cost of

even under the most dire conditions, you're still going to have *some* power going into the system.

Compared with many American homes, of course, I don't require a tremendous amount of power. For instance, my electric car draws 32 amps at 240 volts, or 7,680 watts (about ¾ of a kilowatt) of power. The air-conditioning pulls 18 amps at 240 volts, or 4,430 watts. A lamp with a compact fluorescent lightbulb draws a mere 1.5 amps at 120 volts, or 18 watts.

Besides, having a solar system with batteries for storage means I don't have to worry about brownouts or rolling blackouts or natural disasters. I'm self-sufficient to a very great degree. I sometimes hear from my neighbors that the power has been out for several hours, and I'll have no idea that occurred. And during the 1994 earthquake, for several days mine was the only house in my neighborhood with the lights on and the power functioning.

RACHELLE'S TURN

When I was first living here, Ed would go out of town, and he sometimes would send me running out to the garage to check the numbers on the battery system. And I'd say, "0.6 and 2.10," and he'd freak out and start saying, "Oh, my God! Oh, my God! Switch it up to the grid. But no-no-no. Don't do that first. Switch this one down first."

And then *I'd* be freaking out, because I thought if I didn't do it right, I was going to blow the house up. He'd finally walk me through it and we'd both heave a huge sigh of relief. "Phew. We're safe another day."

Now if I need to switch us over to the grid, it's not such a big deal, but it did take a little getting used to. Come to think of it, maybe it was just the drama of Ed freaking out on me on the phone.

Net Metering

The type of solar electric system I have now *doesn't have to be* connected to the grid, but because I live in an area where it's easy to be connected—and because my house was already connected when I bought it—I have the option of switching over to the grid as needed. *As needed* for me always means after 8 P.M. and before 10 A.M., when power is cheapest due to low demand.

installing a solar electric system. With subsidies, it's eight or nine years—depending on where

There's another way to go that makes a lot of sense, too. Today, instead of having all those batteries at your house, you can choose *net metering.* Many states require utility companies to accept renewable energy from their residential customers. Rather than store any excess solar electricity you produce in big batteries, you can feed that electricity directly into the grid. Then, whenever you need more power than your solar electric system is generating, you simply draw that power back from the grid. In essence, you let the grid itself act like a big battery system for your solar electric setup.

Even if your utility company does not allow for net metering, you can still feed any excess power you produce into the grid. However, instead of receiving the full retail price for that power, the utility pays you a wholesale rate for the electricity, which is considerably less.

Can Anyone Go Solar?

As much as I love solar, let me be clear: Solar panels will not work on just any roof.

A good candidate would be a house with a pitched roof that gets a full day—or close to a full day—of sun. A bad candidate would be a roof that gets a lot of shading from another home or from trees. The western part of your exposure is very important. I have to keep a tree that is west of my solar panels very well trimmed. It's a deciduous tree, so during the winter months, there's very little shading. There are also hedges that I have to keep after quite regularly because they would eventually shade the panels.

Other bad candidates include roofs that are more challenging—a tile roof, for example, or a flat roof. You can certainly put solar panels on flat roofs, people do it all the time, but you want to be very careful that it's done by top-notch installers to prevent leaking. Flat roofs are prone to leaking anyway. When you start putting stuff up there, you have to be very, very care-

you live and how much you pay for power to begin with. With net metering, the power you

ful, both with leakage problems and with the exposure problem. Make sure you get a really good day of sun.

Even before you install a solar system, an energy audit is surely in order to determine how much power you use—and whether you can produce enough power to make the installation worthwhile. You can learn your energy history quickly by reviewing your utility bill. You may also want to implement some of the energy-saving techniques we covered in Chapter 1 so you can get away with a somewhat smaller solar electric system.

Solar for the Midwest?

Now, you might be surprised to hear that my system was not installed by a Los Angeles company. It was put in by Michigan Energy Works.

People say, "Solar's fine for you in California, Arizona, Nevada. These places have a lot of sun. What about the poor people in the Midwest?" I've seen this regularly in newspaper op-ed pieces and stories about solar.

Well, guess what, there's a thriving solar business in the Midwest. Wisconsin. Michigan. Yes, it gets cold there, but it's not cloudy so much of the time as it is in a place like Seattle, where solar wouldn't be as viable. It's often sunny and cold in the Midwest, which is good for generating solar energy. In fact, solar panels lose 15 percent of their efficiency when they get hot, and they don't have that problem in a cold, bright state. On a sunny winter day in Wisconsin or Michigan, those panels are cranking out full current.

Solar is really practical in most parts of the country. If you're not sure about your area, get out the *Farmer's Almanac* and see how many sunny days per year are typical in your area.

Solar Water Heaters

Solar isn't used only to create electricity—you can also install a solar hot water heater. Even if you don't have a complete solar electric setup, there are standalone solar water-heating systems.

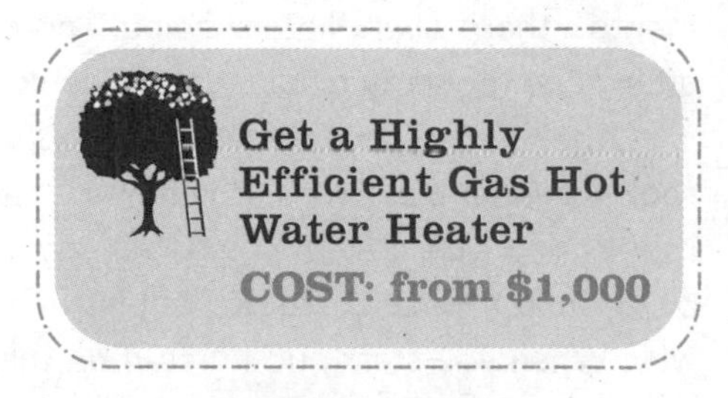

feed into the grid literally spins your electric meter backward. You're selling that power to the

I've got a water heater tank that's hooked up to the solar panels. The sun heats the water, and the hot water gets stored in the tank. Many days when it's sunny out, the water reaches 130 degrees Fahrenheit.

Now, I don't rely on the solar tank exclusively, because you still want to be able to take a shower if it's cloudy for a week—unless you live in a cabin and don't mind being dirty, or you have a wife who's more tolerant of such things. Since I do not, I have a secondary hot water heater that is a standard natural gas unit.

The majority of the time, the solar panels are heating my water, but I've got this superefficient natural gas hot water heater as a backup. It's like I've created a hybrid water-heating system to go along with our hybrid car.

If solar hot water isn't an option, you can get a superefficient Vertex natural gas hot water heater from a company called A. O. Smith. Most standard gas water heaters run at 70 to 75 percent efficiency, and this one runs at 90 percent. It's the most efficient gas water heater on the market.

The Economics of Solar

Let me be clear: I went solar electric in 1990 because at the time I had a TV series and I could afford it. I wanted to do it as a research project, knowing that I was not going to get any payback anytime soon—or at all. I think I just got to the break-even point in 2007—seventeen years later.

Today, you can take advantage of subsidies available in many parts of the country that enable folks to reduce the high cost of installing solar. But back in 1990, there were no federal, state, or local subsidies. I knew I wouldn't amortize the investment until *way* down the line because of how much these systems cost. Don't misunderstand me: My electric bill reduction was *substantial* over those many years, because I got 6½ kilowatts of solar. I reduced my electric bill a great deal every year—and I nearly eliminated it for many years while I was single. That's money saved. But because of the initial upfront costs, it's taken me a long time to break even on this system.

utility company at the exact same price you pay for the electricity you buy. **The sun supplies**

If you want to find out what kind of subsidies are available in your area, look on the Internet or ask a local solar installer. They know these codes inside and out. If you call one to come out and give you a bid, he'll tell you right away, "Here's what you'll get from the state. Here's what's happening now."

It turns out that right now, as we're writing this book, the coffers for solar subsidies in California are empty (we hope to have them filled again soon with the help of the state legislature). But subsidies still exist in other areas.

Even with the subsidies, though, the economics of putting up a solar system like mine have gotten such that you have to be a quarter- to a half-mile away from the grid for it to make economic sense today. If you live that far from real utility power—if you're moving to a cabin somewhere or you're building a house out in the country—you'd have to pay a substantial sum just to get connected to the grid. When you call the local electric company to ask about running power lines out to your home, they'll say, "If you want power out there, we have to trench. We can get a crew out there."

So then you ask, "How much will that cost me?"

"About $35,000 to run a quarter-mile of lines." Or whatever it is.

You go, "Thank you, I appreciate the bid. I'm going to have Fred the solar installer come out, and I'm going to spend $35,000 to $40,000, too. Maybe I'll have a little propane backup generator so I'll never run out of power during a cloudy period. But I'm going to put my money into solar."

I know many people who have cabins who have done that.

Solar Energy for the Masses

Now, $35,000 or $40,000 for a solar electric system clearly is beyond many people's budget. Fortunately, there are some new opportunities that allow even folks on the most modest budget to get into solar.

With the solar electric setup like those I've discussed so far, you buy the whole thing, you have someone install it, and you own it—forever. But now there's another way to go solar that makes more economic sense.

There are companies like Citizenrē that are doing solar panels with a totally different business model. Just like a satellite dish or a cable TV box, you won't *own* the panels. You just want the service and the reliable electricity that comes with them—in this case, a twenty-five-year contract for a fixed

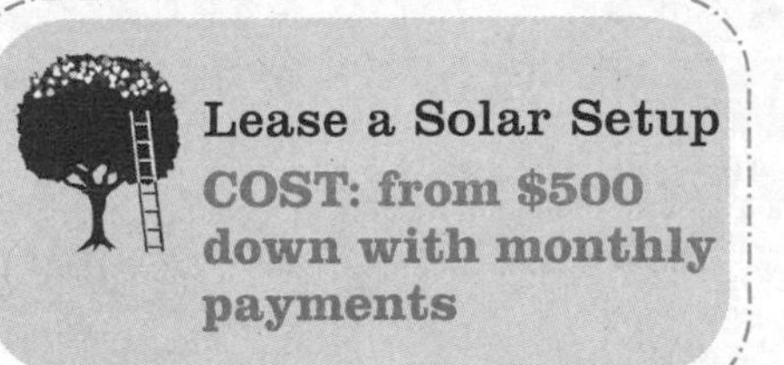

rate for your power, a fixed kilowatt-hour rate. You get the bragging rights of having solar. You get the reliability if there's a power outage that your refrigerator is going to work and that your alarm system is going to work and that your electric gate will open, but you don't *own* the panels.

Why would they ever do this? Because solar panels are so reliable in the long run that after your twenty-five-year contract is up and you decide you don't want to use them anymore, they can install them for somebody else and they're still going to work.

There are companies that are trying different solar business models, and I think they'll be very successful with this. I hope they will be, because why should rich guys who had a TV series in 1990 be the only ones who are able to afford them? There are certainly doctors, dentists, other wealthy professional people who want to do the right thing, and I think it's great and I applaud them, but why should solar be restricted to those demographics? Why can't everybody have it?

I'll let my friend Rob Styler, the president of Citizenrē, tell you more about the benefits of solar energy and how his company works.

Ed's Green Friend: Citizenrē

Is the sun finally rising on solar power?

Way back in 1931, Thomas Edison had a conversation with Henry Ford and Harvey Firestone. Edison said, "I'd put my money on the sun and solar energy. What a source of power! I hope we don't have to wait until oil and coal run out before we tackle that."

Over the last fifteen years, demand for solar energy has increased by 25 percent a year, while prices have dropped an average of 4 percent per year. But despite growing by record numbers, solar systems still represent only 0.01 percent of worldwide energy needs.

Why is this number so low when solar energy is such a plentiful, clean resource? In the past, solar power has been too expensive and too complicated. To switch to solar, people had to take out a second mortgage, invest their children's college fund, or sell their second car to come up with the capital. Then, there's the effort to make it happen—dealing with the installation, maintaining the equipment, getting permits. Who has the time, or the money? Not until solar power can reach parity with utility pricing will more people embrace this option.

Citizenrē has a bold plan to remove all of the traditional barriers to solar power. Our rental offer provides the benefits of solar electricity without the drawbacks: There's no system to purchase. No installation costs. No maintenance concerns. No permit hassles. No performance worries. And no rate increases for the duration of your rental term.

Like most innovations, the Citizenrē model is so simple, it makes you wonder why no one thought of it before. You simply pay a rental fee that is based on the same rate per kilowatt-hour that you used to pay your utility company, with one big difference: Citizenrē guarantees that your rate per kilowatt-hour will not increase for twenty-five years.

With energy costs of all kinds increasing annually, this peace of mind can also save you money. You produce your own power from the sun ***and*** keep the savings every month. We even have a solar savings calculator on our website, www.citizenre.com, that will show exactly how much you can save.

In the past, "going green" usually implied sacrifice. You might feel good about saving the planet, but that good feeling came at a price, as many green products were more expensive than their "dirty" counterparts. With Citizenrē, going green can actually save you money.

State net metering laws make this possible. Through these laws, the grid acts like a huge battery. Your household meter is effectively spinning backward during the day when the sun is shining and forward at night when you pull back power that you have contributed to the grid. These laws were passed because residential energy production is one of the biggest causes of pollution in the United States. For solutions to be sustainable, they need to be simple and make sense on every level, including economic.

Solar power offers energy security, energy independence, no emissions, increased jobs, and economic benefits. Imagine a day when we can power our electric cars from our solar panels and decrease our carbon footprint to the point where each of us can once again tread lightly on the earth.

—Rob Styler

I'm such a big fan of wind power that I've owned half a Zond turbine since 1985.

Wind Power

In Chapter 2, I mentioned that a sailboat is probably the most efficient form of transportation there is—because it's powered solely by the wind. That's not the only way to put this resource to work; wind can be harnessed to generate electricity and power your home.

Before I put a single solar electric panel on my roof, I was already putting ten homes' worth of green power into the Southern California energy system, and I'd been doing that since 1985. Not just enough energy for my house, not enough for two, but ten homes' worth of power.

How did I do that?

By investing in a wind turbine, a portion of a wind farm in Palm Springs, California. Specifically, I own half a Zond, a Danish wind turbine. And that half of a wind turbine has produced enough energy to power ten homes this size—maybe half a home Candy Spelling's size—since then.

If you put a wind turbine—a high-tech kind of windmill—in the right windy location, you can harness that kinetic energy. So the wind turns the blades on a turbine. Then, in most cases, the turbine spins gears in a gearbox (like a car's transmission), and the gearbox turns a generator, creating electricity. It's beautifully simple.

The idea has been around for centuries. Windmills have been used on farms and in rural areas to pump water. The windmill has even become something of a nostalgic symbol of simpler, more bucolic days. Modern windmills can actually bring back some of that bucolic lifestyle. Nobody wants to live next door to a smoke-belching power plant that's burning coal or crude oil, but wind farms are actually quite attractive.

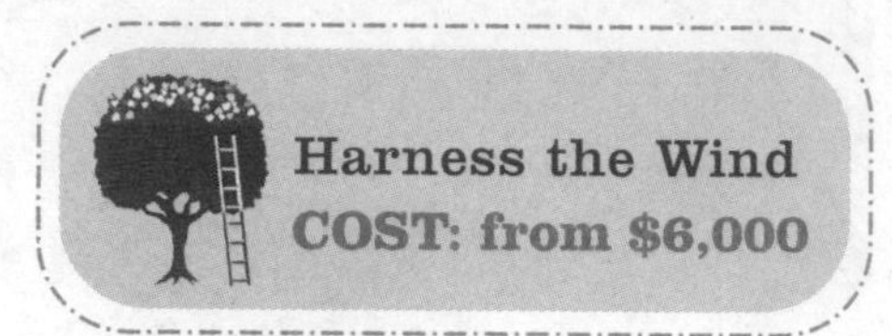

Wind farms also operate pollution free. They don't create *any* harmful emissions that could end up in the air and water, and they don't use up any natural resources, like coal or oil or natural gas. Wind is abundant and free.

Best of all, wind farms can be every bit as cost effective as a modern coal-burning or natural gas–burning power plant.

When I invested in my wind turbine back in 1985, I was no millionaire. I'm not a millionaire now. But if the people who *do* have the dough would do what I did—invest in this clean, green power—that would be the end of coal and nuclear. And by the way, that wind turbine has been a good investment, too.

Residential Wind Turbines

So far, we've been talking about commercial wind farms, also called *large wind.* There's also *small wind,* which refers to turbines that have a capacity of 100 kilowatt-hours or less, and these turbines are being considered more and more for residential use.

Here's how it usually works. The wind turbine provides all—or some—of the power you need for your home, but your house is still connected to the grid. That way you can get electricity from your local utility company during those times when there's no wind or not quite enough. If the wind turbine produces even more power than you need, you can feed that excess power into the grid via net metering—so again, you're literally selling electricity to the utility company.

With this kind of residential wind power system, there's no need for a bat-

enough energy to Earth in *one hour* to supply all of our energy needs for an entire year. How

tery setup like I have at home. But if you install a wind turbine and you're not connected to the grid—if you live in a remote area or if you choose not to connect for whatever reason—then you would need a means of storing power at your home. A stand-alone battery system would provide a reserve for those days when there's not enough wind.

It's very common for wind turbine owners who have totally electric homes—that is, people who have no gas appliances whatsoever—to pay as little as $8 to $15 a month for their utilities nine months out of the year. True, those bills are likely to be higher in the summertime, when the air-conditioning is running, but for three-quarters of the year, they pay next to nothing for electricity, beyond the price of installing the system, of course.

What does this type of system cost? According to the American Wind Energy Association (AWEA), a small turbine can cost anywhere from $6,000 to $22,000 installed, so the investment is not insubstantial. But in several years it will pay for itself, much like my solar electric system has.

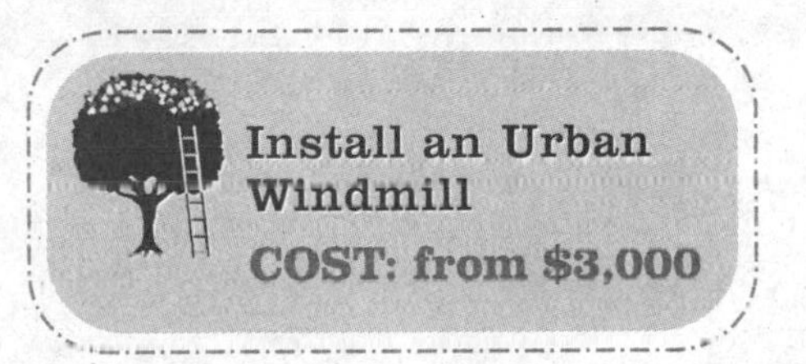

It's important to note that the typical residential wind turbine is not appropriate for every home. These are still pretty large devices, and the rule of thumb is that you need to have at least an acre of land to install one. They're not legal in many more densely populated areas, they can be noisy, and they're not always bird or wildlife friendly. It's like having a giant Cuisinart spinning away in your backyard. To be honest, they kind of scare me.

But now there's another option. A new type of small wind turbine is much better suited to an urban environment, and it's more affordable. It's called a vertical-axis wind turbine (VAWT), and I just installed a 500-watt VAWT on the roof of my garage.

This way I've got solar during the day and then, when the sun goes down, I'm still making energy with the VAWT, which actually runs 24/7. So you could say I've got a true hybrid power system for my home.

I'll let my friend Ken Johnson, COO of PacWind, tell you more about wind power and VAWTs.

do we get power from wind? First, you have to understand that wind is *kinetic energy*, or the

Ed's Green Friend: PacWind

Wind power is, and always has been, the most inexpensive form of alternative energy available to us today. And because of this, it is also one of the fastest-growing segments of the alternative-energy sector. Our winds are ever present, and the amount of wind available to us is infinite. Wind turbines produce zero emissions. They relieve our dependence on foreign oil. They help keep our environment clean for future generations. And they help educate all of us about the need for constant awareness of our fragile environment.

When you think of wind power, you probably picture massive towering structures with swooping blades in our mountain passes and cornfields. This type of wind power comprises the "large wind" industry. This industry supplies clean wind energy to our power grids with the hopes of meeting future demand for power and also the critical need to convert our energy supplies to clean, renewable sources worldwide.

On a smaller scale, when people are looking to rid themselves of their ever-increasing electric bills and to help maintain our environment, they generally utilize a small wind turbine. This is a great way to produce power in rural areas. But to put a sizable dent in our current climate and energy crisis, we need to be able to harness the power of the wind in the populated areas of our world.

Propeller turbines, which dominate the current small-wind industry, have several severe drawbacks that prevent their use in these populated areas, including very high noise levels, instability, and safety concerns. So, then, how do we utilize our infinite supply of wind where we need it the most: in our cities, towns, and backyards?

PacWind has created a full line of revolutionary vertical-axis wind turbines that address this problem. The PacWind designs spin on a vertical axis, rather than a horizontal one, as propellers do, which makes them more adaptable to all types of urban and rural environments.

Our vertical-axis turbines are:

- completely silent
- stable
- safe in all wind conditions up to 100-plus mph
- virtually maintenance-free
- built to last a lifetime

And they can be installed nearly anywhere—around buildings of all shapes and sizes, on homes, boats, bridges, telecom sites, oil rigs, billboards, streetlights, parking lot lighting, and irrigation/water pumping stations. Wherever the wind blows, you can install one.

PacWind turbines can also be stacked vertically in tower configurations where large amounts of power are needed in small amounts of space. We believe these designs will change how we all look at and utilize wind energy. We like to say: Urban wind power has finally arrived.

—Ken Johnson

An Easy Way to Go Green

Say you don't want to make any kind of an investment in your home, even the modest deposit fees involved in leasing solar equipment. Or perhaps none of these options are viable for your location. You can still get greener power into your home—probably through the very same utility company you are now using.

Here's how it works. The local utility company goes out and buys *new* green power in the marketplace. In turn, that company offers you the chance to buy this power for your home.

This is something you can do in most places in the country. You can sign up to buy green power from Austin Energy, or from the Sacramento Municipal Utility District, or from the Eugene Water & Electric Board. You can get it from the Omaha Public Power District or the Iowa Association of Municipal Utilities or Colorado Springs Utilities. Many municipal and public utility companies across the country are offering these green power programs.

Even if your current utility company does *not* have this kind of program, your state may still allow *retail electricity competition.* If so, you can just take your business elsewhere and buy green power from another supplier that does offer the green option.

The good news is that these green programs are introducing *new* green power into the grid. It's not a case of the companies trying to get credit for existing green energy sources—"Oh, we took title to a hydro-plant out in Idaho from 1937. We own it. See? We bought it!"—because then, what's the *new* influence on the grid? That hydro-plant's been cranking out green power for years.

What the LADWP green power program does is put new green power into the grid that we all use. The DWP purchases new wind turbine power. It purchases new geothermal power, new solar power—some kind of alternative power that is clean and green.

Now, there's a little footnote to this: In my area there is an additional charge for taking part in this program.

Originally, the service was offered free to low-income customers; they could have green power for no charge. This enabled the DWP to say, "We have 100,000 homes signed up for this green power program!" They didn't advertise the fact that it didn't cost 50,000 of them a cent, but another 50,000 did sign up to pay an extra penny for every kilowatt of power.

Me, I pay an extra 3¢ per kilowatt-hour because I said, "Look, I heard this green power program is only 20 percent green. I want 100 percent green. Do you have such a program?" And they said, "We'll get back to you."

After a few days, they called back to say it would be a lot of money. I asked, "How much money?" They replied, 3¢ per kilowatt-hour more. Ooh! Three extra cents! I figured I'm using so little power anyway that the difference to my bill would be negligible, so I told them, "Fine. Charge me three cents extra a kilowatt-hour."

Now, remember, I buy nearly all my power off-peak, and that off-peak power starts at less than 4¢ per kilowatt-hour. Even with the 3¢ I'm adding to it for the green power program and some other various charges, I'm still paying only 9¢ a kilowatt-hour, which is very cheap for power. (The average Joe or Jane in California is paying more than 12¢ per kilowatt-hour for the same power.)

So for what little power I use—the less than 10 percent of my consumption for this house, including Rachelle's Pilates studio with the heat on for most of the winter and the air conditioner on for most of the summer, with my larger electric car, with my Begley's Best business, with our daughter and laundry and all kinds of activities—it's still only $600 a year worth of grid power, and all of it's green power. It's green as the solar on my roof. It's just coming from elsewhere.

energy of motion. **According to the American Wind Energy Association (AWEA), a single 5-**

Paying It Back with TerraPass

You can also do something that's very simple—that's just as green and just as real. You can sign up for a carbon offset pass. In Chapter 2 I showed how purchasing these carbon offsets allows you to mitigate the pollution coming from your car and your air travel. Well, you can also mitigate it from your home energy use.

Let's say they don't offer a green power program in the town where you live. You can still have your own personal green power program because you're buying real green power that's really going into the grid from TerraPass or another company like it.

This carbon offset won't stop the pollution being made where you live by the power plant that serves you, but somewhere in the country there's real green power being put into the grid, and that green power offsets the carbon emissions from the power you're actually using.

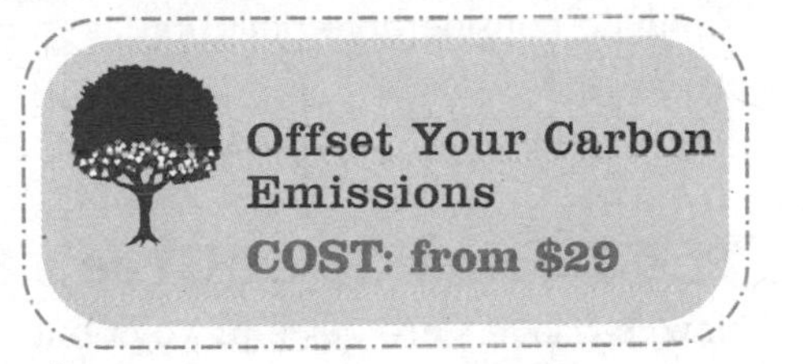

So how do you sign up? You go to the TerraPass website's section on home energy use. They have a screen with different fields. "How much electricity do you use in a year?"

I have no idea. "Honey, give me the bill. Let's see."

You can give me a winter month and a summer month, and there's a way to figure out how much energy you use in a year. I didn't know this, but I use 1,200 kilowatt-hours a month. Who knew? I never knew this, but they asked me to get this information, so I did, and then I typed in "1,200 kilowatt-hours a month."

Next they ask, "Where do you live?" They ask you a few questions.

Then they mitigate. They know by state, by region, the amount of natural gas and coal from your region that you're probably going to use for your power consumption.

They put that into an equation and they say, for example, "For a TerraPass, we're going to charge you $35 a year"—or $135 a year, depending on how much power you use and where you live.

megawatt wind turbine can produce more than 15 million kilowatt-hours of electricity in a

So, as I mentioned in Chapter 2, there're forty thousand people signed up with TerraPass now. What would happen if everybody did that? What if four million people signed up? What would happen then?

I'll tell you what would happen. One by one, utility companies would say, "You know what? Let's shut down that dirty power plant that we're getting all those fines for that's not cost effective to run anymore. We've got all these people signed up for TerraPass. They put up a whole state's worth of green energy in the form of wind. So shut down that coal plant. Did I say one? Shut down two of those coal plants in Indiana that are getting fined."

So yes, there's still real pollution that you're creating by using the power wherever you may be. But then there's also a real offset, which will really eliminate considerable pollution as more and more people sign up. That's just as real.

The Downside of Green Power

Now, naysayers are quick to point out that green forms of power have consequences. And they do:

HYDROELECTRIC POWER. Though totally clean from an emissions standpoint, these big hydroelectric power plants have a cost. They first and foremost prevent many species of fish from reaching their spawning grounds. And then, like the wind turbines, they act as a giant Cuisinart, chopping up fish in their turbines. So they affect the natural habitat of fish and other wildlife.

Now, the hydro-plants recognize this, and they've taken some steps to try to fix the problems. For instance, some utilities have built *fish ladders* to help salmon get past a dam so they can reach their spawning grounds upstream.

The smaller hydoelectric power plants are more environmentally friendly because they do not restrict the flow of a waterway in a manner that is anything like that. The river is allowed to flow and a smaller amount of electricity is harvested in a less restrictive manner.

Homeowners who have rights to a waterway on their property have regularly purchased small hydro units that simply capture the movement of their

year—enough to power more than 1,400 households. Today, U.S. wind farms generate enough

otherwise unrestricted stream. If you had a little stream and you had rights to the water in that stream, you'd install this little paddlewheel-like thing. It's nothing a fish would want to swim into. It would be like a suicide attempt. Like, "Let me go toward that thing that's moving." So a small hydro is much more green.

WIND POWER. Wind turbines can destroy wildlife. You have to site them in a place that's not in the Pacific Flyway, where you have a bunch of birds. You have to—as they have—slow down the blades and change the gearing so you get the same amount of rpm (revolutions per minute) that you need to your generator. You just change your gear ratio, so the blades are going slower. This way, the birds can dodge them better as they're flying through these things that they don't know could kill them. You put reflective coating on the blades so the bird has a better chance. You put up flashing strobes, night and day, so the bird can be like, "Ah! Something bad is there. Let me get away from it." And all these things have greatly reduced the bird deaths.

I'm always thrilled by the output of my stand-alone hybrid solar/wind electric system.

electricity on a typical day to power more than 2.5 million homes. More than six hundred

Now, keep in mind, it's not like birds don't die in smokestacks. Plenty of birds die in "regular" power plants, too. So the people who are highly critical of wind turbines need to remember that there's a consequence for every form of power.

SOLAR POWER. When you make a solar panel, there's gallium arsenide and there're toxic elements, but they're sequestered in a sealed panel. They don't escape into the environment. Maybe when those panels break down—but you tell me when that's gonna be, because I don't know anybody who has a solar panel that's broken. I mean, if you got out there with a handgun and shot holes into it, I suppose you'd have a problem. I can't imagine how you're going to have trouble in the long run with these solar panels. They're pieces of crystal trapped behind pieces of glass or other transparent material on a metal frame. I don't know how that's going to break down.

And there are panels that are still working from the early space program in the '60s. There are solar panels, not just in space, that have been putting out clean, green power for fifty years—very similar to the ones I have on my roof. So they work a long time. And I assume they can be recycled at some point. They can recycle circuit boards. They can recycle lots of other things.

So compare that tiny bit of toxic material in a solar panel with a coal plant that puts out plenty of mercury into the air that we all breathe, that gets into our blood systems, that puts out plenty of other toxic elements and air pollution. The quantities that we're talking about are not even close. It's a teaspoon to a tanker truck.

Now, it's true that solar panels provide electricity only during the daylight hours. That's why God invented batteries—or net metering.

Nuclear Energy

Some people will also tell you that nuclear power is green power. There are renewed discussions of siting new nuclear power plants in many parts of the country as a remedy to global warming. I and many others are not in favor of that due to several factors. One, where do you put the waste? No one—not even the folks in Nevada, who are near the Yucca Mountain Repository—wants it near them. I wouldn't want a nuclear power plant near me.

regulated utility companies in more than thirty states have begun offering green power pro-

Nuclear energy is a devil's bargain. Imagine if the ancient Egyptians had created a poison so toxic that it had just now reduced to half its potency. This material would have been available to every warring nation from that period to this—to fling in catapults, to fling in slingshots, to hide in their opponents' homes or barracks—and we would have had to deal with that poison for the past several thousand years. I don't like the sound of that. I don't think we're capable of having material that toxic available to so many people over such a long period of time. There is tremendous risk.

Then, there's the issue of making more fissionable material available to those who wish to do us harm. Every single nation that has a nuclear *weapons* program started with a nuclear *energy* program.

The risk of a Chernobyl-type accident is also real. Keep in mind that the worst energy-related accident from having solar panels on your roof is that you might get bonked on the head if you didn't bolt down a panel well.

Choosing a Shade of Green

You know, there are different shades of green. Burning biomass is greener than burning coal or burning crude oil. But we must all recognize that it's best to pick the deepest shade of green that is available on our budget and in the realm of common sense.

For you, that might mean installing a solar electric system or a residential wind turbine. Or it might mean signing up for your local utility company's green power program.

And I'd encourage everyone to sign up for TerraPass or one of the other carbon offset programs being offered today, so no matter where your power comes from, you help to add new green power to the grid and help to reduce the need for smoke-belching power plants.

What else can you do to choose a deeper shade of green? You can grow your own food and you can support your local organic farmers.

grams. Getting involved is easy. On your utility bill, check the box: I would like green power.

IN THE GARDEN AND KITCHEN

GROWING YOUR OWN FOOD, BUYING ORGANIC, AND SOLAR COOKING

If you have a patch of dirt to call your own, you can save money by growing your own produce. I grow about 25 percent of the food we eat on my property, and if I had a bigger property, I'd grow even more.

Gardening is great exercise, plus it gives you much more control over the food you eat. You *know* it's fresh and you know it's organic, because you've grown it that way.

There's something about the flavor of produce eaten right off the vine, right off the tree, right out of the garden. Nothing can match a fresh-picked tomato that's truly ripe, rather than one picked green for ease of shipping. The sugar that makes sweet corn so delicious turns to starch in a matter of hours, so even the corn you buy from a produce stand or a farmers' market won't be quite as delicious as fresh picked.

Even if you didn't reap the rewards of your labor in terms of better-tasting food, it's still worth growing your own. It's simply a lot more energy efficient to grow food yourself than to have it shipped long distances.

Today, with supermarkets routinely offering such once-exotic foods as mussels from New Zealand and winter raspberries from Chile, it has become the norm to cook and serve food that has come hundreds, if not thousands, of miles every single day. Obviously, a certain amount of fuel is required to transport food over such long distances. If you can cut down on that, it's a really good thing.

And when you grow your own food, you're using water that's already piped in at your home, not supporting the diversion of millions of gallons to commercial farms' irrigation systems that are far from the water's source. There's an environmental cost to bringing water into your home, certainly, but that water is there in the pipes already. You can collect rainwater to use for watering some of the plants in your garden, too.

Even if you're in a condo or an apartment, you may be able to grow some of your own food. And if you don't have any space where you live, there's another wonderful option: You can participate in a community garden.

You have other choices, too, when it comes to food. When you shop for food, choose food that's organic and buy food that's local. You can also choose to prepare food in an energy-efficient way.

So let's start by looking at what you can grow at home, then get into what you eat and how you cook it.

Why I Garden

When I was a kid I had this thing about self-sufficiency that was born from a very unfortunate mind-set. I was twelve years old when the Bay of Pigs crisis took place and had a profound effect on everyone. We thought that the

The average distance that food travels from field—or ocean or orchard—to table is about 1,300

Nothing tastes better than food that's picked fresh from your own garden.

Russians wanted to kill us, that they were going to send nuclear weapons over to bomb us. We might have been able to stop them, but we might not. And it wasn't just talk. We had duck-and-cover drills at school, and people actually built fallout shelters in their homes and backyards.

So I had a thing about survival and self-sufficiency from an early age. One day my father caught me digging into the foundation of the house. I was going to dig a series of tunnels, then bring down a generator that would run on fuel and that I was going to vent outside. I planned to store the amount of fuel that I thought would be sufficient to run it for a year. I was going to grow algae, which would produce oxygen and also be a food source. In this way I would enable my family to survive the nuclear blast, and it seemed totally sane and rational to think that way. Of course I knew that after the blast there wouldn't be much food around. I'd have to grow it, harvest it, and store it. So I started a garden.

(As a side note, this was actually when I first got interested in solar panels, too. There was no talk about nuclear winter in those days, so I thought I might have some solar panels outside the fallout shelter to provide our

miles. That's the *average* distance. According to the EPA, gasoline-powered lawn and garden

power. Hopefully they wouldn't get damaged by the blast—or I could pull them in and then put them out afterward. And I'd live. I'd survive.)

My love of gardening wasn't solely about providing sustenance in the wake of a nuclear disaster, though; I simply liked the idea of the earth. I had been a Boy Scout—thrifty, brave, clean, reverent, resourceful. Gardening fit with all of that and I wanted to give it a try.

I started my first garden at my home on Magnolia Boulevard in Sherman Oaks when I was sixteen. And right after I put some seeds in the ground, my dad told me, "We're going to New York for a visit, and we're going to be back there awhile." And then when we got to New York, he decided we were going to Europe. We took a whirlwind twenty-one-day tour of several countries in Europe. It was wonderful in every way.

When I came back, though, I thought, "Oh, my God! My garden!" I had been gone maybe six weeks.

But miraculously, several of the plants had survived. They weren't in great shape, but some water overspray from the neighbor had been enough to take care of a few radish plants, and the radishes were kinda edible. I was impressed beyond description. Those seeds I had put in the ground, and tended to only briefly, had endured absolute neglect for six weeks and still produced radishes.

I vowed that I would again have a garden when I had a patch of dirt to call my own. So the number one thing I wanted for this house when I bought it was room for a vegetable garden, and it has turned out I am good at gardening.

Eco-Friendly Gardening

You know, when I first bought this house, the garden was quite different. I knew enough to take the lawn out right away. It just didn't make sense to have a lawn in Southern California. If I lived in Seattle or Indianapolis—any part of the country that gets a certain amount of rainfall—then I might have been comfortable having a lawn, but I

equipment, on average, produces 5 percent of the ozone-forming VOCs in areas with smog

certainly wouldn't have one in a place like Southern California, where water comes at such a high environmental cost.

Getting rid of a lawn can also do wonders for the environment. First of all, you could entirely eliminate the need for gasoline-powered lawn equipment at your home. By that I mean things like lawn mowers, edgers, and string trimmers. These machines emit all kinds of pollutants, including

- carbon monoxide
- carbon dioxide
- oxides of nitrogen (NO_x)
- sulfur dioxide
- VOCs (volatile organic compounds)
- toxins, such as benzene

There's also gasoline evaporation whenever you refill your gas can and whenever you use that gas can to refill your mower or edger. And If you don't maintain your equipment properly, it can burn oil, too.

Choose Plants Suited to Your Site
COST: from $1 or less

One of the keys that I've learned over the years to having a successful, energy-efficient garden is choosing plants that are suited to my site. If you live in the desert, as I do, plants that thrive in moist, tropical climates are not going to be happy unless you give them lots of water and lots of special fertilizers and generally try to adapt your site to suit the plants. This is virtually never an environmentally enlightened way to approach your garden.

Plants that have adapted to your climate and conditions are better able to grow without a lot of attention or input. In my case, that means native plants from this region as well as plants that are classified as Mediterranean.

You can check with your local garden center or your local county extension office to find out which plants will work best in your climate and conditions. If you're in California, you can go online to the California Native Plant Society's website (www.cnps.org) and find lots of good stuff. Odds are there's a native plant society in your state or region, too

problems. The oxides of nitrogen and sulfur dioxide released by lawn equipment react with

Over the years I've developed a list of produce that grows well for me and that I plant year in, year out:

- corn
- tomatoes
- lettuce
- broccoli
- cauliflower
- peas
- artichokes
- chile peppers
- onions
- herbs like cilantro, basil, and sage

I also have a little fruit orchard at the front, back, and side of my house where I have these trees:

- 2 avocado trees
- 1 lemon tree
- 2 semidwarf tangerine trees
- 1 Valencia orange tree and 1 semidwarf navel orange
- 3 fig trees
- 2 olive trees (I cure my own olives)
- 1 large apple tree and 2 semidwarf ones
- 1 plum tree

With many of these plants, the more you cut, the more you get. Broccoli is like that. Sometimes I can't even cut it quick enough, 'cause you can only eat so much broccoli.

It's not like I have a huge amount of space. I have three raised beds, and the whole area where those three raised beds sit is only about 25 feet by 35 feet, including the walkways in between. There's another little area that adjoins it that's maybe 3 feet by 6 feet. So, obviously, you don't need a lot of space to have a thriving fruit and vegetable garden. You just need to use the space efficiently, and to choose plants that will thrive in your climate.

water in the atmosphere to form acid rain. **It's much easier—and much more environmentally**

One Tree Goes a Long Way

RACHELLE'S TURN

Ed's always telling me we could live off the land, and I guess it's true. If there's a little space, he wants to put in a fruit tree. I didn't exactly plan to live on a farm when I moved to California—that wasn't my big, glamorous dream—but I do have to admit I can tell the difference between our fresh vegetables and that bland, tasteless stuff. My dad and my grandfather had a garden when I was growing up in the South and it was incredible. Fresh collard greens. What a fresh tomato tasted like, not having been sprayed with pesticides and not having had all the flavor mutated out of it. It's a beautiful thing.

So there's a lot to be said for having fresh, organic produce, even if your garden produces far more artichokes and broccoli than you'll *ever* want to eat. And if you do have too much of a good thing, you can give the extra fruit and vegetables to your friends and neighbors, donate it to a local shelter, or maybe barter with other people for goods and services. Hey, if you grow enough of this stuff, you could maybe even sell it at a farmers' market.

Rachelle's right about the kind of bounty you can enjoy. A single semidwarf apple tree, for example, can produce up to five hundred apples in a season, and that one tree has a productive life of fifteen to twenty years. If you live in a temperate climate, like California, you can plant several trees with different harvest times—so one might produce fruit in March and April, and then another might produce in May and June. That way you can wind up putting fresh-picked fruit on your table for much of the year.

Wherever you live, make sure you choose trees that work well in your climate. For instance, in the far north, you can grow hardy apples and pears. A bit farther south, try sour cherries, plums, and apricots. And in the nation's midsection, add regular cherries, nectarines, and peaches. Of course, citrus fruits can be grown in some areas of the South. Just bear in mind that most fruit trees require a dormant period, when temperatures remain below 45 degrees, so if you live in the Deep South, check with local nurseries for low-chill varieties.

Even if you're unable to add a tree to your home, by getting rid of the

friendly—to choose plants that are native to your area or that are native to an area like it.

lawn and adding native or climate-compatible plants that don't require extra energy and water and fertilizer, you can reduce pollution and also absorb carbon dioxide and release oxygen.

Also, whether or not you plant trees at your home, you can work with local and nationwide organizations to plant trees in local parks and literally all over the world—to beautify our land and to help the environment.

Drought-Tolerant Ornamentals

Not everything in my garden is edible. There are a few ornamentals, which are strictly decorative, but none of them really requires very much water. We live in a desert, so it doesn't make sense to have it any other way.

Some people assume that means I have a cactus garden. Not at all. The drought-tolerant plants in my garden include

- lavender, which smells wonderful
- manzanita
- toyon, which is also called Christmas berry
- ceanothus, or California lilac

Rachelle also put in a succulent or two in the back.

RACHELLE'S TURN

Does planting drought-tolerant natives mean you have to have an ugly garden? Well, when I first moved in, I used to tell people that our house was the one on the corner that looked like the Addams family's. We had all these crazy-looking plants out in the garden and it looked sort of barren.

Now that things have grown in, it does look better. It's no Sissinghurst, believe me. It's not some gorgeous castle garden that people come from all over the world to tour. But I'd be willing to have people over for a garden party now.

Actually, the amazing thing is that people *do* want to come and tour our garden. People have actually paid money at auctions held during fund-raisers for different environmental charities to come and visit Ed. They actually pay money to see the house and tour the

Choosing the right plants for your garden is good for your pocketbook, too; by planting varie-

drought-tolerant garden that produces some of the food we eat. It's absolutely unbelievable to me. I told Ed we should start charging admission at the gate.

Saving Water in the Garden

Even when you plant the right plants for your climate, you will occasionally have to water them; even drought-tolerant plants have their limits. So the idea is to avoid wasting water. As I mentioned in Chapter 1, "Home," saving water also means saving energy—and saving money.

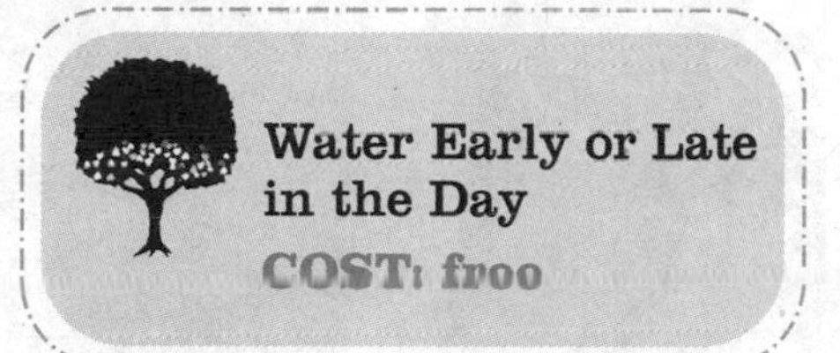

What are the best ways to save water in your garden? You'll use a lot less water overall if you water early in the morning or later in the evening, so the hot midday sun doesn't make that water evaporate. Also, try to water when it's not windy so the water goes where you want and doesn't simply blow around the garden or into a neighbor's yard.

What else can you do? You can collect rainwater to irrigate your garden, literally capturing water off the large watershed that is your roof. Rain barrels make this easy, and they're getting easier to find. Your roof has a large amount of surface area, and it's focused in sometimes as few as four downspouts. Position a rain barrel under one or more of those downspouts and you can capture the rain as it comes down off your roof.

You'd be surprised how much water you can collect this way. If it's raining hard, you'll fill up a 55-gallon rain barrel—with 300 to 400 feet of surface area leading to one downspout—in just an hour or two. And you can certainly put up multiple barrels. I had to fight tooth and nail to get just one rain barrel, since my wife has aesthetic issues with it. And the only reason it's still there is that it's full of water and she can't move it.

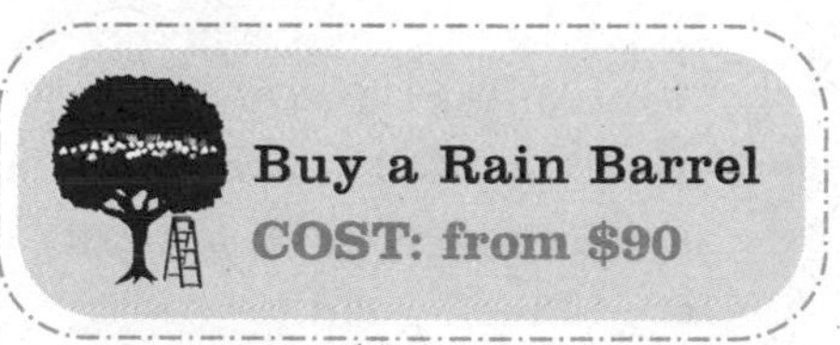

ties that don't need a lot of watering, you will be keeping your monthly water bill lower.

Ed rigged up this ugly rain barrel, but it is kind of handy for watering my ornamentals.

RACHELLE'S TURN

Every time I leave the house, I risk coming back to some weird contraption. In this case, Ed had cut one of our rain gutters and installed this horrible, ugly orange barrel. I can live with some things. I can actually live with a lot of things. But they have to look good.

Ed tells me he's found some more attractive rain barrels, even some made out of stone. I don't know if the man can be trusted when it comes to aesthetics; he clearly has other priorities. But if he's found an attractive rain barrel, I'm all for it. I don't want to waste water out in the garden, especially when rainwater is free.

If you have 600 square feet of rooftop, nearly 375 gallons of rainwater would hit your roof for

Of course I understand why Rachelle says that these orange rain barrels are ugly, but to me, the sight of the Owens Valley—about 250 miles from Los Angeles, where we've robbed the area of the water and the dust blowing around is giving the residents respiratory ailments—is much uglier. And if you put it that way, Rachelle would probably even agree.

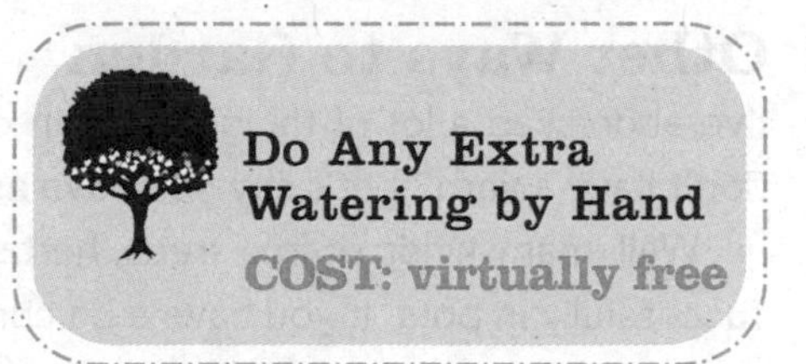

If you can irrigate your ornamental plants with saved rainwater, you will cut your water bill considerably. And if your wife takes long showers, well, then you really need to look into this rain-barrel system.

The other thing you really should do, if you're going to use rain barrels—or just as part of your regular home maintenance—is get up on the roof and clean the rain gutters. You want to make sure the water you collect in your rain barrels is as clean as possible, and cleaning the gutters of leaves and other detritus will definitely help. We've got four feral cats living on our roof, so God knows what else is up there. But getting rid of the leaves is a good first step.

You'll want to position the rain barrel on some stones or even make a platform if you're handy, but remember it has to be quite substantial; that barrel is going to get very, very heavy when it's full of water. The idea is to position the rain barrel high enough so you can get a bucket underneath the spigot, which is down at the bottom.

When you're ready to use that water in your garden—or if the barrel is nearly full and more rain is predicted—open the spigot and drain some of that collected rainwater into another container or two, or twenty.

It's important to point out that this water shouldn't be used for drinking. It's not potable—and you might even want to put a sign on the barrel to this effect, so you don't get sued by anyone. Certainly if you have cats living on the roof, as I have, you should be very careful. By the same token, unless you're sure it's very clean water, you wouldn't want to use it on anything that will be eaten, so don't water your vegetable garden with it. You'd have to have a very clean area to collect rainwater to use it on food. Instead, use it for watering your ornamentals or your lawn, if you still have one.

each inch of rainfall, enough to fill close to seven 55-gallon rain barrels. There are an

Other Ways to Garden

I've addressed a lot of things you can do in your own yard, but what if you don't have a yard? Let's say you have an apartment or a condo.

Well, many kinds of fruit trees, herbs, and vegetables can be grown very successfully in pots. If you have a balcony or a patio or even just a front step that gets some sun, you can grow a surprising amount of food.

If you've got a south-facing window, you can also grow some cherry tomatoes indoors, as well as some types of herbs.

A lot of people have rooftop gardens, too. That's another great way for city dwellers to grow food.

Start a Rooftop Garden

COST: from just a few dollars

And if you want to garden on a larger scale, you can become part of a community garden. They've got them all over. There are community gardens in cities including

- New York
- L.A.
- Fresno, California
- Chicago
- Fairbanks, Alaska
- Huntsville, Alabama
- Boulder, Colorado
- Hartford, Connecticut
- Atlanta
- Gainesville, Florida
- Indianapolis
- Des Moines

And if there isn't one near you, start your own. A group called Urban Farming (www.urbanfarming.org) helps people around the nation start community gardens.

Here's how a community garden works. Essentially, the city donates the plot of land, usually an unused lot in a developed area. They may say, "This is

estimated eighteen thousand community gardens throughout the United States and Canada.

an old Department of Water and Power lot that we don't use anymore. We're going to give this to people to grow food." There's a ribbon-cutting ceremony and a whole big thing.

Everyone who signs up for an allotment is given an area that's maybe 20 feet by 30 feet to tend and plant in whatever way they choose. You can grow food there or flowers or whatever you want. There's water available to you, but you do have to bring in your own soil amendments. You can make compost at home or on-site.

Gardening for Health

I do want to mention that gardening isn't just good for my pocketbook. And it isn't just good for my taste buds. It's also good for my health:

- Gardening provides both a strength-training and a cardiovascular workout. Anyone who's ever carried a couple of full watering cans or pushed a wheelbarrow knows this.
- Gardening increases flexibility.
- Gardening provides exactly the kind of exercise recommended for the prevention of heart disease, high blood pressure, obesity, and adult-onset diabetes.
- Gardening helps prevent osteoporosis.
- Gardening relieves stress and helps you to live in the moment.
- Gardening also allows you to express your creativity, and that's good for your brain and your spirit.

The healing benefits of simply being in a garden are well documented, too. For years, hospitals have had healing gardens.

Gardening has even been used as a type of physical therapy for people with special needs or for those who are recovering from injuries. It's been shown to improve eye-to-hand coordination, range of motion, motor skills, and even self-esteem.

Healthy trees—and other plants—absorb carbon dioxide and release oxygen, so they're

Gardening is also a great way to meet your neighbors. Hang out in the front yard for a while and soon you'll find you are experiencing a real sense of community.

I've also come to see that gardening is a wonderful way for parents to connect with kids (even grown children). I learned a lot about the cycle of life by gardening as a child, and you can teach your kids about everything from delayed gratification to the benefits of cleaning your tools and putting them away properly every time.

So why wouldn't you take a little time to create your own sanctuary that just so happens to have the benefits of providing delicious fresh food and reducing our energy needs?

Gardening for the Environment

I've touched on the environmental drawbacks of having to ship food an average of 1,300 miles. Clearly, a lot of fuel is burned and a lot of emissions are created in that process. But there are other environmental reasons to start your own garden, particularly if you choose native plants. Gardens make the air healthier for everyone, humans and animals, in your neighborhood, and they keep the ecology of the area in better balance.

Inviting birds and other animals into your garden not only provides valuable habitat for these creatures—who are often getting crowded by continuing development in our cities and suburbs—but also enables nature to provide its own form of pest control.

Beneficial insects will do the work of pesticides, so you don't need to introduce poisons into your garden. Praying mantises are a perfect example. They won't eat your plants, but they will eat the small insects that do, including beetles, caterpillars, and aphids. You can buy them as well as ladybugs for your garden. A single ladybug can eat as many as five thousand aphids in its lifetime, which is about a year.

Yet another environmentally friendly way to control small pests, like white flies, black flies, and aphids, is to mix up some soapy water and spray it directly on

literally cleaning the air we breathe. They also filter water, prevent soil erosion, help retain

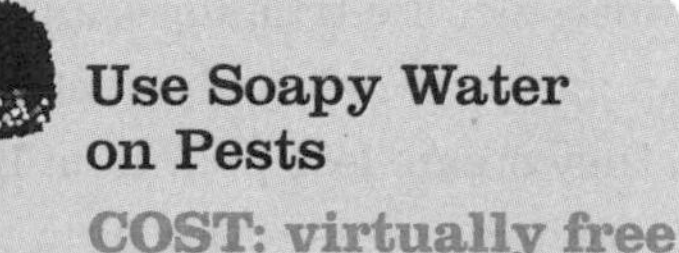

Use Soapy Water on Pests
COST: virtually free

these bugs. Even a good, hard stream from the hose can shake these pests loose and discourage them from attacking plants in your garden.

If you've got snails and slugs, there's still no need to get out the poison. Instead of using pesticides, you can find snail traps at your local home and garden shop. You might even try experimenting with beer traps. And then when it's time to dispose of these slimy creatures, you can simply submerge them in salty water.

Of course, insecticides aren't the only poisons you'll want to avoid. It's also important to avoid herbicides—that is, poisons that are designed to kill plants. Rather than poisoning the weeds in your garden, take a few minutes and pull them out by hand or with simple garden tools.

Also, you can use mulch—or plant drought-tolerant groundcovers—to reduce the number of weeds that come up in the first place. Many people have a habit of raking up every single leaf that falls in their yard. Leave some of those leaves to turn into mulch. You can even use grass clippings in your flower and vegetable beds to help hold in water and reduce weeds. Then, as these clippings and leaves break down, they provide nutrients to the soil, so you'll need less fertilizer, too.

Pull Weeds, Don't Poison Them
COST: free

Silent Gardening

I've touched on the problems associated with gasoline-powered lawn equipment, but you may not be willing or ready to give up on the lawn entirely. I do keep a small lawn area along my parkway—that access strip by the curb, where people have to walk and kids cut through on their way to school. If you want to keep at least a small patch of lawn, or if your spouse insists on it, is there another way to maintain those small lawns—and the rest of your yard—without using gasoline-powered equipment? Absolutely.

groundwater, and provide homes for wildlife. A typical lawn mower can be as loud as 95 to

- **Use electric equipment.** Electric mowers, electric trimmers, and electric blowers are more energy efficient than gas-powered equipment. They require less handling of gasoline and they create less pollution. If you have a solar-powered house, or you're buying green power from the many utilities that offer green power, you'll be creating *a lot* less pollution than if you were using that horrible two-stroke engine that most lawn mowers use. Electric equipment also makes less noise, so there's less noise pollution.
- **Use rechargeable equipment.** Battery-powered leaf blowers are much quieter than two-stroke equipment yet are still quite effective.
- **Use manual tools.** Even better than electric or battery-operated tools—for small yards or small jobs—are hand tools. The only energy they need is the energy you expend while using them. This includes push mowers and—dare I suggest it?—good old-fashioned rakes.
- **Reduce mowing time.** If you replace regular turf grass with another type of grass that's designed to grow long, like mondograss, you can reduce the need to mow—maybe even as infrequently as once or twice a year. The same goes for planting a prairie-style meadow instead of a lawn. You just mow it once at the end of the season and wait for it to come up again on its own in the springtime.

I'm really lucky to have found a gardener who understands this stuff. While I'd love to do all my own gardening, I've gotten so busy lately that I need help taking care of all my plants and trees and shrubs. Fortunately, my friend and gardener Chris Houchin owns a company called Quiet Garden Landscaping. I'll let him explain how he has reduced wasted energy and water—as well as noise—in my garden.

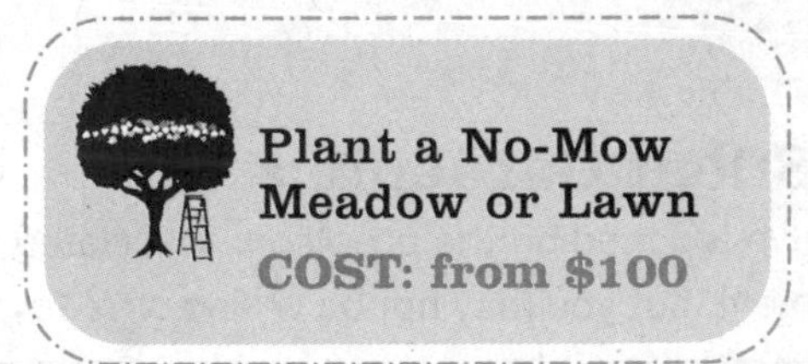

Ed's Green Friend: Quiet Garden Landscaping

I first met Ed at the local hardware store, where he was delivering a shipment of his Begley's Best natural cleaning solution. He hired me on the spot to maintain his property after learning that I use only conventional manual, electric, and battery-powered gardening tools. These tools include a rake, a 24-volt cordless lawn mower, a rechargeable weed whacker, an electric weed whacker, and yes, two different kinds of noncombustion leaf blowers.

The Cordless Broom, which I use instead of a gasoline-powered leaf blower, can run 10 to 13 minutes on one fully charged 18-volt battery. It's more than adequate for clearing walkways, porches, and similar surfaces of dust and debris. It creates zero emissions and creates about as much noise as your hair dryer.

The electric weed whacker requires an extension cord and a standard 110-volt outlet. It has quite a bit more power—and unfortunately makes more noise—than the cordless variety, but is still much quieter than any two-stroke engine. Yes, running an extension cord can be a bit of a "drag," but once you get your system down, it's not that big a deal. Besides, I mostly use it in the autumn when there is a tremendous amount of organic debris to collect.

I could go on and on about the ill effects of gas-powered leaf blowers on mothers, newborns, elderly people, people with asthma, and night workers—and the stress they cause to our friends in the animal world. On top of that, many communities now have city ordinances banning the two-cycle leaf blower, which gives off as much smog as seventeen cars. The bottom line: Blowers are bad!

Other tips: If one plant or one area needs some extra water, there's no need to water everything around it. Just bring a hose to hand water that particular plant, or set up a drip line so water is concentrated directly on the root system.

New plants also need more water than plants that have become established. You'll find that established drought-tolerant plants may need only one or two good soakings each summer.

—Chris Houchin

What Is Compost?

Every good gardener sings the praises of compost, but what exactly *is* it? At the most basic level, it's an organic material that contains humus—dark brown or black material that looks like superrich soil and has a pleasant, earthy smell.

Creating compost really is mimicking what occurs in nature, where biological decomposition happens all the time. As leaves fall off a tree and plants die, they slowly decay. That decomposed plant matter is full of nutrients and minerals, and it feeds the soil beneath it, helping to continue the cycle of life.

You can re-create the same process in your own backyard—and you can make it happen faster than it does in nature.

WHY COMPOST?

Composting is good on so many levels:

- **Landfills.** Composting keeps organic materials out of landfills, reducing the rate at which landfills reach their capacities. So it reduces the need for more landfills.
- **Energy and pollution.** Composting also reduces the amount of trash that needs to be picked up and transported to landfills, so it saves energy and reduces pollution from all those garbage trucks driving through our cities.
- **Methane gas.** Composting reduces the production of methane gas in landfills, so it also reduces pollution in that way. In other words, composting is a very good thing for the environment and for the world as a whole.
- **Saving money.** On a more personal level, in your own garden, composting is wonderful, too. Composting will save you money in a lot of ways. For one, you won't need to go out and buy fertilizer—or at least not nearly as much.
- **Weeds.** You won't need to worry as much about weeds and plant diseases, since applying compost to your beds is beneficial for your plants and your soil, and it suppresses the growth of weeds.
- **Higher yields.** You also will get more from your plants—more fruit,

100 decibels, and a gas-powered leaf blower can register 95 to 105 decibels. When it comes to

more vegetables—since composting adds nutrients to your soil.

- **Saving water.** Using compost helps to keep moisture in the ground, which means you can water less.
- **Cleaning your soil.** Composting has been used on a large scale to help remediate contamination at all kinds of cleanup sites. Studies have shown that compost will bind to contaminants (including heavy metals) in the soil, preventing them from running off into the water supply—and preventing them from being absorbed by your plants, and therefore the fruits and vegetables you're going to eat. If a former resident did something nasty, like dump used motor oil out in the yard, compost can help make that area usable again.

How's that for reaping a lot of benefits from stuff you were going to throw out anyway?

HOW TO START YOUR OWN COMPOST PILE

The first step in getting a compost heap going is accumulating material to be composted. I keep a 5-gallon pail with a lid on it just outside the back door. You can keep it in the kitchen if you want, but make sure the lid has a good seal; you don't want to attract cockroaches or ants or other pests.

I use that pail to collect all my day-to-day kitchen scraps that are not animal based—that is, things that are not meat or dairy. I include things like

- breakfast: banana peel, coffee grounds, tea bags
- lunch: scraps left over from the salad or whatever you were making
- dinner: those scraps and ends from vegetables, all of the ends from broccoli stems, all the ends from any onions chopped up or any vegetable, the brownish outer leaves, the wilted part of anything

Create Your Own Compost
COST: free, if you just make a pile, or from $25 for a compost bin

I collect all that stuff in a big bowl as I cook and take it outside to the pail. Then, once a day, I

composting, brown materials are high in carbon, while green materials are high in

I love turning kitchen scraps—trash—into rich, nutritious compost for my garden.

empty that bucket into the next container, which is my large compost container. These come in a lot of different shapes and sizes. It can be a compost bin. I have a large bin that's 50 gallons or more. But it could also be a compost drum that you turn with a handle, or even just a pile in your backyard.

The important note: If you do decide to start a compost *pile* in your backyard and you don't have a lid on your compost, you must cover it with dirt regularly. You can't have raw melon rinds out there and different scraps in plain view, uncovered, or you will attract lots of pests that you don't want, including cockroaches, raccoons, maybe even rats.

What you do want to invite into your compost are beneficial critters: earthworms, grub worms, friendly bacteria, and fungi. They're going to break down the matter that you put out there in your compost pile or bin or drum.

And you do that by getting the right combination of nitrogen and carbon. Fortunately for me and everybody else, you don't need to know the exact

nitrogen. For the best compost, maintain a ratio of 50/50 brown to green material. **In 1980,**

ratio of nitrogen to carbon. The way to achieve that ratio without remembering the number is simply to have your compost be half green and half brown, and to keep it wet. Just put in layers, half green and half brown.

What do I mean by green? By green I mean:

- green grass clippings
- green plant matter from the garden, things you trim off while doing your gardening activities
- green weeds you've pulled
- green table scraps, like the ends of broccoli and lettuce
- seaweed and pond algae count as green materials too, if you have a pond

By brown I mean:

- grass that has wilted or gone brown
- plants that have gone brown and wilted and died
- brown leaves
- pine needles
- shredded twigs
- straw or sawdust (though you'll need to avoid sawdust from wood that has been treated with chemicals)
- shredded paper—it can be good to add some shredded newspaper to your compost from time to time

Keep your compost moist, but not soaking wet, and turn it occasionally. If your composter is a drum, you just turn the handle. If it's a bin or a pile, get out the shovel and turn over the materials manually.

Over time, by some miracle of nature, you will have roughly the right ratio of nitrogen to carbon, and you'll have great compost.

Remember that when we're talking about kitchen scraps, you can't compost meat or any bones. You also can't compost most animal waste, at least not from carnivores, because it contains pathogens and stuff you don't want around your food.

On the other hand, if you have herbivores, like bunnies, you can add their waste to your compost pile. In fact, animal waste from herbivores can be a

the United States Department of Agriculture (USDA) defined organic farming as a system that great way to get your compost really hot right away—in other words, to get that matter decomposing quickly. It's like starting a yogurt with a specific culture. To start compost, to get it really hot right away, go to a pony ride and get some horse manure and put that in. Boom! Your compost gets fired up right away. Cow manure and chicken manure work, too.

The funny thing is, there won't be any smell from this stuff, because you'll cover the animal waste right away. It'll be in the center—at the core—of your compost pile, making everything start decomposing really quickly. And you'll have usable compost for your garden in as little as a month.

Eat Organic

If you follow all the steps and suggestions in this chapter, and don't use any chemical fertilizers or other products on your plants, you'll be an organic gardener. But what about the food you buy? As I said earlier, I grow only about 25 percent of the food I eat, so when I'm out shopping for that other 75 percent, I buy organic whenever it's available.

At one time, the term *organic* was quite loosey-goosey. *Organic* could be just a marketing phrase that a company decided to put on its packaging. That ended when the USDA introduced a stricter definition of the term and regulations for its use.

In 1990, the Farm Bill made it possible for the USDA to develop a national set of standards and certification criteria, and it also allowed the agency to come up with some labeling directives for organic foods. Those standards were released in April 2001, so now the USDA essentially has control over what is or is not called organic, and it can enforce those standards.

There are many, many reasons to opt for organic foods, but perhaps the most compelling one is that organic food naturally tastes better. That's because flavor is the result of lots of different and complex molecules. Healthy, living soil provides a constant and more complex mixture of these molecules, which results in more flavor. It's like how winemakers are always talking about

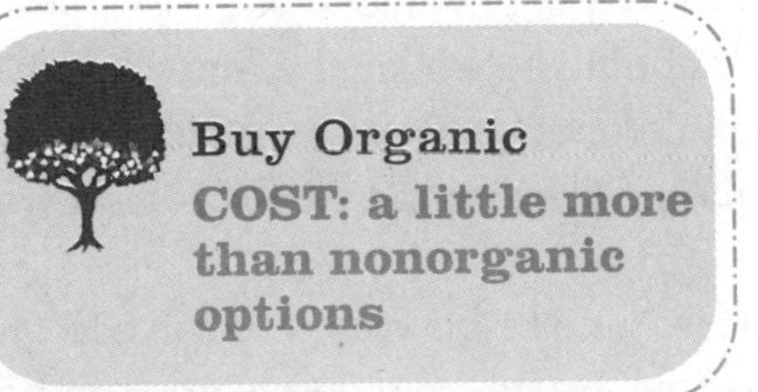

excludes the use of synthetic fertilizers, pesticides, and growth regulators. Organic agricul-

the importance of *terroir,* about the soil and the climate and the general environment in which the grapes are grown. Well, it doesn't only matter with grapes. It matters with all food.

Clearly, over time, organically grown food is best for us, the environment, and future generations. And it's big business now, too.

So I buy organic. The other thing I seek out are non-GMO foods, foods that have not been genetically modified. I think that that's a very dangerous experiment. The possibility of allergic reactions, toxins, and digestive problems that can develop make me quite leery of things that are genetically modified. I avoid them at all costs.

Opt for Foods that Are Produced Locally

I also make every effort to support local farmers. After growing your own food, buying food grown locally is the next best choice. If you live in a more rural area, you know that local farmers often sell fresh produce from stands on their property.

Since I'm in a more urban area, I visit my local farmers' market just about every weekend. There's probably one near you, too.

Farmers' markets gather local vendors with a variety of products in one place at a regular time, such as every Saturday from 8 A.M. to noon. You can pick up all the fruits and vegetables that you can't grow in your own garden, as well as things like organic meat and eggs, nuts and dried fruits, and freshly baked bread. Some markets also offer things like beeswax candles, organic yarn, and beauty products. Farmers' markets are also a great place to get ideas of what to plant yourself, since these fruits and vegetables are grown locally—which means there's a good chance these plants would thrive in your garden.

By purchasing from a local vendor,

ture is better for the soil and the ecosystem in which the crops and the livestock are raised.

- you're helping reduce the energy used to truck food from faraway places to your local grocery store, as well as the need for packing materials
- you're getting food that's much fresher—often picked the same day (In contrast, produce in the grocery store may have spent one or even two weeks in transit.)
- you're getting food that was grown for its taste, not for its ability to survive being machine-harvested and shipped hundreds, if not thousands, of miles
- you're often helping support smaller farm operations, including local mom-and-pop farms
- you're keeping your money within your local economy, which is good for your community

For those times when I can't grow my own food or buy food that was grown locally, I make every effort to buy fair-trade food. Fair-trade farmers not only receive a living wage for their labors, but are also encouraged to engage in sustainable farming practices.

You can find all sorts of imported food that is labeled "fair trade," including the following:

- coffee
- tea
- chocolate
- cashews
- olive oil
- rice
- sugar
- hearts of palm
- salmon
- honey
- salsa
- jam
- syrup

The market for organic products worldwide is now valued at $28 billion. There are more than 4,300

Why I'm a Vegetarian

If I seem to be more interested in fruits and vegetables than the average American male, there's a good reason for that. I became a vegetarian for the first time in 1970.

I did it for a number of reasons. I had seen some photographs and films about conditions in a slaughterhouse, and it just seemed like a really bad thing to be subsidizing that culture. It wasn't like the old days, when Farmer Jim would raise a cow on the side of a hill, then, at the end of its bucolic life of grazing, being nestled, having calves under a tree, he would slaughter it. Perhaps the farmer and his family would say a prayer, as the Native Americans do, for the life of the cow. It isn't like that anymore. Cows are confined in really horrible conditions, the worst kind of conditions, for their whole lives, and the way they are dealt with is quite unsavory.

So I became a vegetarian for the cruelty issues involved with cattle raising and chicken farms and hog farms and all that—and I also did it for my health. I'd heard it was better to incorporate more plant food into your diet, and that movement grew in popularity in 1970, so I decided to try it. Some people take to it, some don't, but I responded really well to eliminating meat from my diet. I haven't had red meat since 1970, and I feel really good.

Of course, you don't have to be a vegetarian to eat more fruits and vegetables. Filling up on greens rather than meat actually helps the environment.

There are six billion of us on this planet. The amount of arable land has essentially remained static over the years, but the population has risen exponentially, so the amount of arable land per person has actually dropped. Eating lower on the food chain helps save water and energy, and it also requires less land for farming. Just as an efficiency expert, removing any compassionate issues from the discussion, I can say that being a vegetarian makes a lot of sense.

The funny thing is, many people use vegetables to make their meat more palatable. I've been told by meat eaters, "I don't know how you can eat those vegetables. I eat meat, and it's delicious and it's wonderful."

"Really? You just have a raw steak?"

"No, I put on some ketchup or salsa." And they have their tacos with lettuce and tomatoes and olives and onions. They cook their roasts with onions and carrots and celery to add their flavors.

farmers' markets held regularly in cities all across the United States. **It's more land efficient,**

I make lots of easy, delicious dishes with fresh vegetables and organic seasonings.

So I have to ask, “Do you want that meat to taste more like vegetables?” Okay, yeah. As for me, I’ll just have my vegetables taste like vegetables, thank you.

Now, some vegetarians don’t want to have things that taste like meat. They want broccoli. They don’t want anything to taste like pork or veal or anything. That’s why they’re vegetarians.

But if you like the taste of meat, you can eat vegetarian foods that are quite healthy. They’re vegetables spiced with other vegetables, and they taste just fine. And there are different soy products that mimic both the taste and texture of various meat products, such as bacon or ham.

In the early ’90s, I discovered I was lactose intolerant, so I took my vegetarian diet a step further and became a vegan. No dairy, no chicken, no eggs, no fish.

I feel a lot better since I’ve stopped eating dairy, both because I wasn’t entirely comfortable with the conditions for the animals at many dairy farms

water efficient, and energy efficient to grow plant-based materials than to raise animals for meat;

and also because dairy was making me sick. I had a sore throat all the time when I was consuming milk and cheese and other dairy products. I was practically living on the stuff.

I wasn't able to remain entirely vegan, though. In 2001 I started eating salmon once in a while. I do the cooking in the house, and one day when I was making a piece of salmon for Rachelle, I realized it looked really good to me. I was craving it in a deep, deep way. I thought, "Okay, I'll try it. Maybe I'll get sick. It's been nine years since I've had any fish. How has my digestive tract adapted to a totally vegan diet?" I didn't get sick at all, and I felt very good. So I guess I can blame my lapse from veganism on Rachelle.

At this point I'm 80 to 90 percent vegan, and once in a while I have a piece of salmon. Go figure. But I feel good.

Home Cooking—or Not

I used to cook all the time, but between my Begley's Best business, our TV show, and my acting career, things have been kind of busy and I rarely find the time. Consequently, we're eating out quite a bit.

It's easier for a vegan to find restaurants to eat in now than it was years ago. A restaurant called the Vegan Plate recently opened near me and it's so good I could eat there twice a day and be happy.

But I do have breakfast and lunch at home. A really quick lunch would be some vegetarian sushi; Whole Foods makes a wonderful avocado roll and a vegetable roll. Occasionally I get Amy's frozen enchilada plates. They're very, very good and they're quick, so if you're in a rush, you can cook and go.

But there's a tendency—and I'll be honest with you, I'm disappointed to see it in myself all too often—to rush our meals. In response to this unfortunate (and unhealthy) trend, a movement that started in Italy and spread throughout Europe has reached the States. The Slow Food Movement is meant to provide an alternative to our fast-food culture, and it encourages folks to savor their food, to enjoy the process of preparing food, and to take their time with their meals. I think that's a laudable goal that we should all pursue. We can all slow down and not be quite so busy.

When it comes to dinner, we don't always eat out. I may not cook, but we often buy healthful prepared stuff and serve it at home. (Of course we recy-

it simply takes a lot more land and water and energy to raise a pound of beef than it does to

cle all the packaging.) But when I get the chance, I still do like to get in the kitchen and cook—even if my "kitchen" is sometimes my own backyard.

Solar Cooking: The Backyard Without a Barbecue

People would probably be surprised to hear that I don't have a barbecue grill. A barbecue burns charcoal and releases nasty emissions into the atmosphere. Instead, I have a solar oven.

We certainly have heard the bad side of the greenhouse effect, where we might be heating up the planet at a rate that is inconsistent with a long lifespan. The very good side to it, for us, is without the greenhouse effect, we'd be very cold. We would perish because we wouldn't have that warmth that is provided by that greenhouse effect. And a solar oven makes use of the greenhouse effect in the best possible way.

I've been using a wonderful solar oven for years. It's essentially an insulated box with a pane of glass to retain the heat, sealed very nicely. It also has reflectors—from the north, south, east, and west—placed at a 45-degree angle to focus that light into the box even better. That makes it a hot, hot box. I built a rolling stand so I can move the oven around throughout the day to capture the maximum sun, and I even bought a second solar oven so now I can cook more things at the same time.

If you stop and think about it, you need a temperature of only 212 degrees Fahrenheit to boil water, to make soup, to make rice, to make beans. That temperature is easily achievable and sustainable for long periods in a solar oven.

I have found, however, that there are some things I cannot do in my solar ovens. I can't sauté, and I can't really bake well because for baking, you need 400-plus degrees. On a really good day, I get 375 degrees in my solar oven, but when I put in a cold mass of flour, water, or whatever to bake, that temperature plummets down to 200 degrees for a time before it eventually comes back up. That results in some pretty leaden baked goods.

But the things a solar oven does do, it does exceptionally well. I find it also keeps foods moister—and it holds in the flavor—far better than a gas or electric oven.

RACHELLE'S TURN

That solar oven used to be the bane of my existence. I'd come out into the backyard and it was in one position, then I'd come back out and—boom—walk straight into the solar oven. It turns out Ed was always moving it strategically around the backyard so it would be in a position to get the most sun.

For years I considered that solar oven a real eyesore. They say beauty's in the eye of the beholder, and obviously Ed will always find it beautiful. I would never call it beautiful; functional, I suppose, but unattractive (although if you stand by it, with all those reflectors, you can get a nice tan).

And it does work. In the morning he'll put some water in it with some potatoes and vegetables, and by the afternoon, it's soup or stew. He makes all sorts of dishes with it. I think he likes the novelty of it.

I especially like the fact that it's essentially free food. He mostly uses stuff we've grown on-site, and we're using the free power from the sun to cook it. So that part's good, even if I do have to watch my step in the garden. Besides, the stuff Ed makes actually tastes good, so I guess I shouldn't complain. At least he doesn't make me do the cooking!

Ed's Cooking Hierarchy

Just as I do for modes of transportation, I have a preference ranking for cooking methods. Raw foods, like salads and many other wonderful fruit and vegetable dishes, don't require any energy other than what is used to bring the water for rinsing and cleanup, but other dishes do require cooking, and that generally requires energy.

Obviously, when I can, I cook in my solar ovens as much as possible. That would be my first choice.

After that comes electric. There are quite a few things I can cook with electricity, especially if you use the word *cook* to mean making a hot beverage like a cup of coffee or tea, because that's made in my electric teakettle.

there's no additional energy required for cooking. Cooking in it is free, and eco-friendly.

The last line of defense for me is the precious resource known as natural gas. Natural gas burns pretty clean, and I have a natural gas stove and a natural gas oven, as most people do, so I cook that way when I have to. What I don't do is burn wood or charcoal or propane in a barbecue grill. Wood and charcoal burn very dirty. Natural gas burns cleaner, but it does not even come close to being 100 percent clean, like a solar oven. So the choice to barbecue doesn't exist in my cooking hierarchy.

Ed's Favorite Recipes

After seeing a *Living with Ed* episode where I cooked in my solar oven, many people wrote to request the recipes for the dishes I prepared. I've included those recipes here, along with a few more of my favorites.

Ed's Lentil Soup

4 cups water
1 cup lentils
1 medium onion, chopped
1 medium carrot, chopped
10 broccoli florets
1 teaspoon chopped ginger
1 tablespoon chopped garlic
½ teaspoon chopped serrano or jalapeño pepper, with seeds
1 teaspoon salt

Either on a conventional stove or in a solar oven, in a large pot, bring the water to a boil. Add the lentils, onion, carrot, broccoli, ginger, garlic, and hot pepper. Stir, return to a boil, and cook over medium heat for 45 minutes, or until the lentils become soft.

Stir in 1 teaspoon of salt, and serve. Enjoy!

SERVES 4

Ed's Vegan Birthday Brownies

- $\frac{1}{4}$ cup vegetable oil, plus more for pan
- 8 ounces soft to medium tofu
- 1 cup raw sugar or honey
- 2 teaspoons vanilla extract
- $\frac{1}{4}$ cup cocoa or carob powder
- $1\frac{1}{3}$ cups whole wheat pastry flour
- 2 teaspoons baking powder
- $\frac{3}{4}$ cup chopped pecans

Preheat the oven to 350°F. Lightly oil an 8 × 8-inch cake pan.

In a blender or food processor, blend the tofu, sugar or honey, vanilla, oil, and cocoa powder until smooth and creamy.

In a large bowl, sift together the flour and baking powder. Add the pecans and tofu mixture to the flour and mix together gently until just combined. If the batter is too dry, add a splash of water.

Spoon the batter into the prepared pan and bake for 20 to 25 minutes. Test with a knife to see if it's done; it should come out clean with just a few moist crumbs when inserted in the middle.

Cool in the pan for 5 minutes before cutting into squares.

MAKES 6 LARGE BROWNIES

Ed's Spicy Thai Basil Eggplant

1-pound eggplant
2 tablespoons brown rice vinegar
1½ tablespoons brown sugar
1 tablespoon soy sauce
1 serrano chile pepper, minced, with seeds
3 tablespoons toasted sesame oil
3 garlic cloves, minced
3 tablespoons chopped Thai basil
2 tablespoons sesame seeds, toasted

Preheat the oven to 425°F.

Slash the eggplant in several places so it won't explode and place it on a baking sheet. Bake for 30 minutes, or until soft when pressed. Remove from the oven and let the eggplant cool for 15 minutes.

When the eggplant is cool enough to handle, peel off the skin and chop the flesh into sugar cube–size pieces.

While the eggplant is cooking and cooling, in a small bowl, mix together the vinegar, sugar, soy sauce, and chile peppers.

Heat a wok over high heat and add the oil. When the oil is hot, add the garlic and cook for 30 seconds. Add the eggplant to the hot oil and cook for 2 minutes, then add the vinegar mixture and cook for 1 minute longer.

Remove from the heat, stir in the basil, and top with the sesame seeds before serving.

SERVES 6

Ed's Olives

You need to cure at least a quart or two to make it worth your while.

Fresh (uncured) olives
Rock salt
Olive oil
Vinegar or fresh lemon juice
Garlic (optional)
Herbs, such as thyme, rosemary, oregano (optional)

Wash the olives well, remove the stems, and soak them in a jar of water for 3 days, changing the water every day.

When they have soaked for 3 days, drain the olives. Return them to the jar, adding a layer of 4 tablespoons of rock salt after every 3 cups of olives. Cover the jar with a lid and shake gently to mix the salt and olives.

Turn and shake the jar every day, draining off any excess liquid. After 8 or 10 days, taste the olives to see if they're still bitter. If they're not, they're done. At that point rinse the olives and set them aside.

Bring a large pot of water to a boil. Add the olives and boil them for 5 minutes, then drain.

Put the cooked olives in a jar with a few spoonfuls of olive oil and a sprinkle of lemon juice. You can add slices of garlic or herbs to suit your taste. The olives should be stored in a refrigerator and turned or shaken once a week.

And One from Rachelle

RACHELLE'S TURN

I'm not much of a cook. That's more Ed's department. But when I do feel the need to create in the kitchen, I have one dish that's always a crowd-pleaser. I bake salmon in aluminum foil with some lemon juice and spices. It's a poached salmon, and it's really moist. Everyone—including me—loves it and thinks it's delicious. And even better, it's supereasy.

Rachelle's Poached Salmon

I'm a person of excess, so the more garlic, the more pepper, the more everything, the better. And then, occasionally, for an Asian variation, I'll skip the dill and instead use ginger and scallions and garlic to season the salmon.

1 pound (about 4) salmon fillets
2 lemons
1 tablespoon chopped fresh dill
1 garlic clove, minced
Salt to taste
Freshly ground black pepper to taste

Preheat the oven to 375°F.

Tear a piece of aluminum foil that's at least twice as large as your salmon fillets. Place the fillets in the center of the foil and fold up the edges of the foil around the fish, creating a basin.

Squeeze the lemons over the fish and distribute the dill and garlic more or less evenly over the fillets. Season with salt and pepper.

Bring the edges of the foil together over the fish fillets and fold the edges over several times to seal. Place the packet in a deep pan and bake in the oven for 10 to 15 minutes. When the salmon starts to flake, it's done!

SERVES 4

RACHELLE'S TURN

Being an actress in L.A.—just being in L.A.—there's a lot of pressure to look perfect, to be thin and stay young and beautiful forever. It's a struggle. The makeup, the skin-care regimens, the Botox—if there's some serum out there that will make me look ten years younger but will kill me ten years faster, I might have to get back to you on that. My rational mind would say it's crazy, but my L.A. mind . . .

Even with all that pressure and the many temptations, I don't diet. In fact, I eat almost everything. Instead of adhering to strict rules, I exercise and eat a balanced mix of foods including lots of whole grains, lean protein, fruits, and vegetables.

In my opinion, the best way to maintain a healthy weight is to control the size of the portions you eat and to be aware of your calorie intake. As long as you burn as many calories as you eat, you can stay fit and healthy.

Eat Well, Live Well

It's so obvious that you're going to feel better eating the freshest, most healthfully prepared organic food that's available to you. And there's nothing better than that sense of satisfaction that comes from eating food you've grown yourself.

It also feels wonderful to get to know your local farmers—whether at a farm stand or at a farmers' market—and to support their organic practices and support their local businesses.

You can do so much good for yourself and your community in that way. And you can do so much good for the world as a whole by growing trees and other plants, by cutting down on the distance food has to travel to your table, and by reducing the use of chemical poisons.

When you do buy things from a greater distance—especially from an underdeveloped country—you can choose to buy things that are fair trade.

You can also make much the same choices when it comes to clothing and hair- and skin-care products. You can choose to buy organic and buy local and buy fair trade. And you can choose to stay away from harmful chemicals and to be kind to your body and the environment.

CLOTHING AND HAIR AND SKIN CARE

6

ALL THE THINGS YOU PUT ON YOUR SKIN

Even people who are very aware of the food they eat—people who make it a point to eat only fresh, organic food—often aren't aware of the choices they have when it comes to clothing and hair- and skin-care products.

In fact, most people just don't realize the significance of things like organic clothing and organic shampoo. It sounds kind of out there, like some kind of crazy New Age stuff. But it's not only what you put *into* your body that matters; what you put *onto* it matters just as much, too.

RACHELLE'S TURN

I used to think Ed was just being Ed about all this stuff. What's the big deal? But then I learned that the skin is our body's largest organ, and because it's porous, it's absorbing stuff all the time. If medicine can be applied to the skin—hormone patches and that sort of thing—just imagine what else your skin is taking in. Studies on the effects of toxins in drinking water have actually found that people took in more of the toxins by *showering* in the water than by *drinking* it!

So contact with your skin—for ten, fifteen, maybe twenty hours in a day—is a big part of why the clothes you wear matter so much. And it's not just your clothes, but all your lotions and shampoos and makeup—not to mention the air we breathe. Everything that comes in contact with your skin matters.

If you stop for just a minute and think about it, the same principles that apply to organic gardening and organic farming clearly should apply to the growing of crops used to make clothing and hair-care and skin-care products, too. Pesticides that are harmful to food and the ecosystem are just as harmful when they're used on nonfood crops like cotton and lavender.

And then there are the synthetic materials used to make everything from clothing and shoes to makeup and sunscreen. Manufacturing these materials requires a lot of energy and natural resources—including problematic resources like petroleum—not to mention all the emissions from the manufacturing processes.

So there are real, measurable consequences for the environment—as well as for our bodies—when you choose what to wear and what to apply to your skin and hair. For that reason, it is doubly important to choose carefully and wisely when you shop for clothes and beauty products.

"Conventional" Clothing

If you've spent any time reading the labels on your pants and shirts and sweaters or dresses, you know most clothing these days is made of one or more of these materials:

Don't assume that natural fibers are automatically better than synthetics. Just because some-

- cotton
- nylon
- spandex
- silk
- wool
- polyester
- acrylic
- linen
- rayon
- acetate
- cashmere
- angora

Some of these materials are natural and some are synthetic. By definition the natural materials are found in nature and include cotton, silk, wool, linen, cashmere, and angora.

Cotton and linen both come from plants. Cotton obviously comes from the cotton plant—specifically, from fibers in the plant's seedpod. Linen comes from fibers in the stalk of the flax plant.

Silk, wool, cashmere, and angora all come from animals. Silk is made from the cocoon of the silkworm. Wool is made from the fur of animals including sheep, goats, alpacas, and llamas, while angora, a specific kind of wool often used to make soft, furry sweaters, is made from rabbit fur. And cashmere is made from the cashmere goat's fur.

Those are the most commonly used natural materials, and they are widely available. However, many fabrics combine natural fibers with other, synthetic fibers to give them more durability or other qualities. Many of the synthetics—including nylon, spandex, polyester, and acrylic—are petroleum-based thermoplastics. Plastics! They're man-made substances manufactured in a lab, and they all contribute to our dependence on foreign oil.

Rayon and acetate are a little different from the other synthetics. They're actually made from cellulose, which is wood fibers, so rayon and acetate will feel more like natural fibers, such as cotton or linen, but they're still manufactured fibers that require a lot of water and energy to produce.

So which are the most environmentally friendly clothing choices? The answer is not always obvious.

Growing Cotton

Most people think of cotton as a sort of friendly fiber. It breathes. It's washable. It comes from a renewable resource. If we need more fabric, we can just grow more cotton, right?

thing is made from natural fibers doesn't mean it's environmentally friendly. **The pesticides**

RACHELLE'S TURN

I always wondered what the big deal was about organic cotton. Cotton is cotton, right? It wasn't until very recently that I learned cotton is one of the most toxic plants on the planet—not because of the plant itself, but because of the boll weevil, a virulent pest that infests the cotton plant. Boll weevils are very hard to kill, and cotton farmers have to use all these pesticides to protect their crops. Eventually weevils become immune to a pesticide, mutating around it, like a cockroach, and the farmers have to find a brand-new pesticide. They keep adding pesticides and making them more intense until you have a crop with more pesticides used on it than anything else out there.

Rachelle's right. Cotton is one of the most pesticide-laden crops in the world.

The obvious problem with pesticides is that they're poisons. Moreover, they're typically not highly targeted poisons, particularly those used in the growing of cotton. These pesticides work more like a shotgun blast than a sharpshooter's bullet when it comes to killing insects. Instead of just killing the boll weevil, these pesticides wind up killing spiders and wasps and all kinds of other beneficial insects, putting the entire ecosystem out of whack. Eventually you have aphids multiplying like crazy and wreaking havoc on the cotton, because their natural predators have been destroyed, which in turn requires *more* pesticides.

Sadly, they work like a shotgun blast when it comes to their application as well. Thousands and thousands of farmers and farmworkers and children and animals have been made seriously ill—and have even been killed—by pesticide poisoning, even when the pesticides are applied in a way that's 100 percent legal. When you're flying an airplane over a field and dousing it with toxic chemicals, just a bit of a breeze can carry those chemicals for many yards or possibly miles. Even if you have people walking through the fields and spraying the pesticides directly onto the crops, those pesticides can be deadly for farmworkers as well as wildlife.

And it gets worse. Where does that pesticide go when the cotton field gets watered, or when it rains? Does it wind up in the streams? Does it wind up in the water table? Of course it does.

applied to plants don't just target insects; they may also encompass an *herbicide,* which kills

Does some of that pesticide wind up in the clothing made from that cotton? Probably. Most of it gets washed away as the fiber is cleaned and milled, but then where does that wastewater from the cleaning process go?

The bottom line is this: Why put all that poison out there?

Organic Cotton

Fortunately, organic cotton is a good alternative to pesticide-laden cotton. Organic cotton is just like organic broccoli. It's grown without the use of synthetic pesticides, with attention to the ecosystem and biodiversity and the health of the land and the wildlife around it. By wearing organic-cotton clothes you are ensuring that you aren't walking around in clothes full of residual pesticides, and you're not supporting the introduction of more chemicals into the ecosystem. That's why I always look for organic-cotton clothing.

Sure, it costs more. But how much more? A buck? Two? For a T-shirt that I'll be wearing next to my skin for many years, even if it's an extra five bucks, it's worth it to me.

I consider it a very promising sign that some of the biggest retailers on the planet have gotten involved with organic cotton. Through its suppliers, Wal-Mart is fast becoming the biggest buyer of organic cotton in the world, buying more organic cotton in a single year than was sold *worldwide* just a few years ago. And you know if it's being sold at Wal Mart, it's not expensive, so the cost factor is no longer an issue.

Organic Clothing

It's important to point out that organic clothing is not just limited to cotton. You can also find organic clothing made from:

- hemp
- ramie
- jute
- bamboo
- silk
- wool

plants, or a *fungicide,* which kills various types of fungus. **If there's an item of clothing you**

All of these fibers are natural, and all except silk and wool come from plants. Naturally, the plants would have to be farmed organically in order for their fibers to go into organic clothing.

Of those plant-based materials, hemp has been the most controversial. For years it was banned in the United States because *Cannabis sativa,* the plant whose stalk yields hemp fibers, also yields dried flowers and leaves that are better known as marijuana. Yet hemp is such a valuable fiber for making everything from rope to clothing that our Founding Fathers actually required people to grow hemp back in the 1600s. Today, organically grown hemp has become a staple of the organic-clothing industry.

Another natural fiber is jute, a relative of hemp that's commonly used to make rope and twine and burlap sacks, as well as carpet backing and, to a lesser degree, clothing. Ramie, from the ramie plant, also known as China grass, is used to create a fabric that feels much like linen. And bamboo is a wonderful material. It's one of the most sustainable resources, and it can be used to create a soft, silky fabric.

As for the animal-based materials, organic silk—or what's sometimes called peace silk—is gathered from wild silkworms after the moths have emerged from their cocoons. Organic wool comes from sheep (and other animals) that have been raised in a sustainable, organic fashion.

While there is no official standard for labeling clothing *organic* just yet, most organic-clothing manufacturers—I won't say *all,* but I sincerely hope all of them—also avoid the use of hazardous chemicals during the manufacturing process. By this I mean things like dyes and other chemical treatments that come in contact with the workers in the factory—and with your skin when you wear the clothing.

Whenever I buy new clothes, I always look for organic fabrics. I can't find absolutely everything organic yet, but I always make a real effort to look for organic clothing of every kind. Does that mean you and I should throw out all our old nonorganic clothing? Of course not. Why would you fill a landfill with perfectly usable stuff?

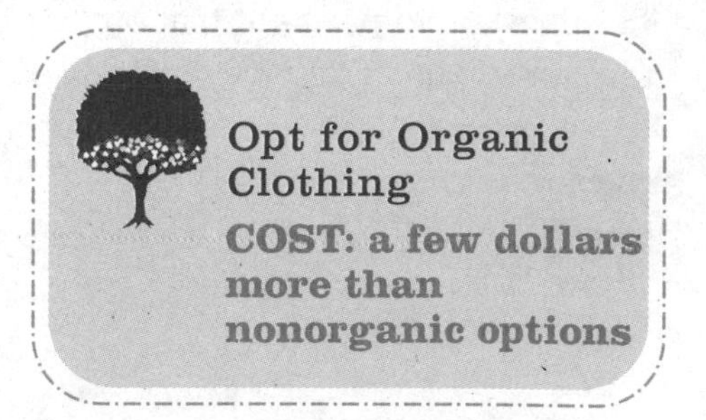

hardly ever need, why buy it and have it sit in your closet, unused and practically wasted, when

I still have some old, nonorganic T-shirts that I'll wear until they fall apart. And when they do fall apart, I'll probably use them as rags so they can have a second life around the house or out in the garage.

Shorts and T-Shirts: Simplicity Is the Answer

I'm a simple guy, and I keep my wardrobe pretty simple: shorts and T-shirts. If it's cool out—or if I've got the heat turned way down to save energy—then I throw on a flannel shirt over my T-shirt. Of course, I'm in Southern California, so I'm not dealing with snow and sleet and ice on a regular basis.

But I've really made a conscious choice to keep my wardrobe—and my life—simple. And because I choose to wear simple styles, it's easy to find organic clothing that suits me.

Occasionally, I have to wear a suit. If I have to go to a Hollywood event, a premiere or an awards ceremony or some fancy-dress occasion, I wear one of the suits I bought in the '80s and early '90s that still fit me. These suits are old, but they're well made and they're wool. I'll probably have them for a few more decades. (As I mentioned in Chapter 5, I'm mostly vegan. Some vegans won't wear wool, but just as I eat some salmon once in a while, I do also wear wool. It's my personal choice.)

When it is time to buy a new suit, there are eco-friendly choices. In the '80s, it was nearly impossible to find business suits and tuxedos and dressier clothing made from organic fabrics, but it's much easier now.

I also keep a suitcase packed and ready at all times. (Soldiers in battlefield conditions always have their packs ready to go; I've got my suitcase.) The suitcase is taking up space in my closet anyway; what better place to store a few T-shirts, some socks, and some underwear and toiletries than where they will surely next be used? This way I'm ready if I get a last-minute acting job or a speaking engagement. If someone calls and says, "Can you leave right now?" I really can.

you can rent it for far less money and allow other people to make use of it, too? Leather

Green Style: The Fashionable Compromise

RACHELLE'S TURN

I love clothes and shoes. I think I'm actually a borderline shopaholic. However, I'm all about comfort *with style.* Most days, I wear stylish casual wear, like a fashionable T-shirt and jeans.

Several nights a week Ed and I go out, and I'll put on something a little more elegant. Even then, though, I like to be comfortable. There's nothing worse than wearing a nice dress and tugging at the straps all night. I want to know that I'm going to be warm enough and I'm not going to be complaining about my lower back because my heels are too high. Having been a dancer and having hurt my body, I know the importance of good shoes, so I look for stylish shoes with lower heels.

I love fashion, but I'm not a slave to it. The most important thing about all my clothes is that they fit. If it doesn't look good on my body, I won't wear it. I know my body type and what colors look good on me.

Color is important to me. I love blues and spring and summer pastel colors because I'm a blond, blue-eyed, fair-skinned person

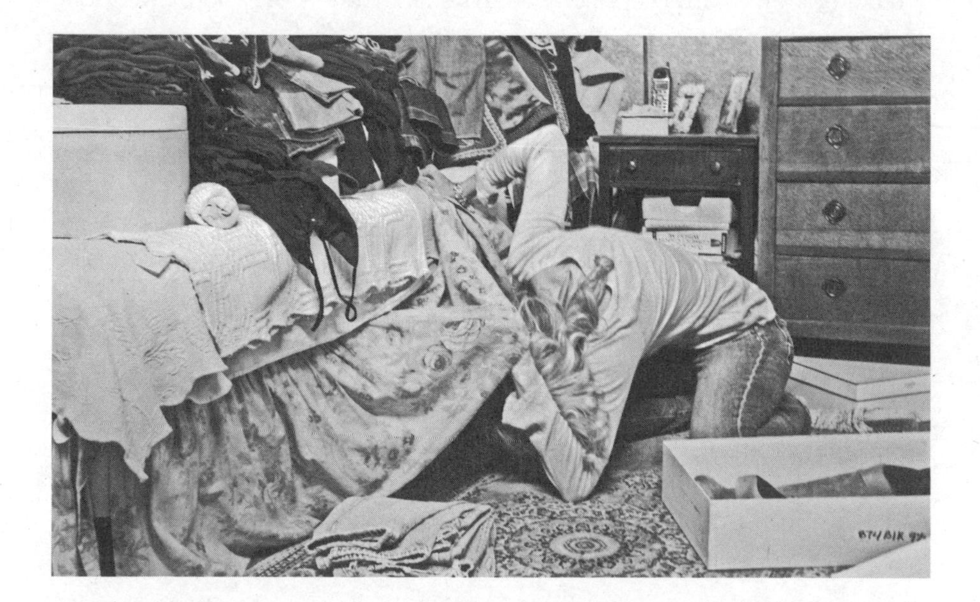

production involves a toxic soup of chemicals, many of which have been linked to all kinds of

and those colors just look better on my skin. Of course I also tend to wear a lot of black, because every designer does black. Most people look good in black, so it's a great option. If not, try navy or gray.

Until very recently I would have never considered "green" clothing. It was not even on my radar. Why should I bother to go that extra step to wear organic?

Now, of course, I know the difference between pesticide-laden cotton and organic cotton. And then there's the sustainability factor with the clothing manufacturer. How do you get your fabric? Is it fair trade? Those things are important, and they're becoming much more important to me.

But style is important to me too, and many of the organic fashions I've come across are either Pacific Northwest or grunge or hippie-granola-girl style. I like a little more tailoring. For me the new frontier is finding eco-friendly clothing with a more couture attitude so I can know my clothes are created in a way that won't hurt me, the people who made them, or the land—and are still the most stylish looks of the season.

For years, Rachelle would complain about organic clothing styles—or the lack thereof. But now a few designers are starting to use organic fabrics and create genuine couture, the kind of stuff fashion magazines feature not because it's organic, but because it's real fashion. As with anything, there's a learning curve. Designers and manufacturers are having to figure out which fabrics will work for which styles. They have to research the way a material will hang, not to mention how it will wear over time and hold up to cleaning. And when we're talking about some of the newer materials, like bamboo and coconut fiber, being used to make clothing, you can appreciate the steepness of the learning curve.

Rachelle used to complain about clothing made from hemp. She said it was too rough. But now fabric manufacturers have been able to blend it with silk or with organic cotton to make it more wearable. Advancements in the whole dye and fabric world are happening all the time, too. As demand for these organic fashions increases, we'll see more money being spent on R&D.

cancers and other health issues, including asthma. Many dry cleaners have found that

Rachelle is actually working with a friend to design her own clothing line. I think it's great. It's a passion of hers, and if it can help the environment, too, I'm all for it.

Recycled Clothing

In Chapter 3 I talked a lot about the importance of recycling, and I touched on the value of purchasing recycled furniture—whether you're buying antiques, thrift-shop bargains, or items made from reclaimed materials. Recycled clothing fits into the same category.

When you purchase something that already exists, you're saving natural resources and all the energy used to mine or harvest them, to ship them to a manufacturing facility, to transform those raw resources into finished goods, then to transport those finished goods to warehouses and retail stores.

So, what do I mean by *recycled clothing*? I mean preowned clothes and also clothing made from recycled materials.

You can find preowned clothing—and shoes—in all sorts of stores and in all sorts of styles. Thrift shops, flea markets, and swap meets are great sources of inexpensive clothing that isn't ready for a landfill—it's ready for a new life in *your* closet. If you're looking for something more upscale, some thrift shops do specialize in higher-end merchandise, or you might try shopping in a consignment store (sometimes called a resale store). These stores specialize in preowned designer apparel.

Another excellent option is clothing made from recycled materials. Some of the designers working in the organic clothing realm are using vintage buttons, so they're recycling in that sense. Other companies are taking cool vintage clothing—sweaters, dresses—and remaking it in more current styles and sizes. Rachelle was telling me about companies that take old cashmere from sweaters and blankets and scarves and that sort of thing and recycle it into new clothes as well as scarves and quilts.

But scarves aren't the only recycled accessories you can find. Some pretty

making the switch to green processes wasn't just good for their health, it was good for their

impressive—you might even say mind-boggling—purses are made from all kinds of recycled materials, including automobile seat belts, license plates, bicycle inner tubes, vinyl records, 35mm slides, blue jeans, soda cans, old soda can pop tops, juice boxes, candy wrappers, skateboards, and magazines.

When you buy recycled clothing and shoes and purses, you're keeping all of these items out of landfills *and* you're reducing energy use and the use of natural resources.

Rental Clothing

Another great option, in terms of conserving resources (not to mention money) is renting.

What sort of clothing can you rent? For men, tuxedos are certainly the best-known rental option. But you can also rent a business suit for a job interview, say, and if you won't actually need that suit when you start working, renting it makes a lot of sense.

The same goes for ladies' clothing. How many times do you really plan to wear your wedding dress? Once, right? So why buy it, wear it once, then have it take up space in a closet or up in the attic for the rest of your life? Oh, and you can rent prom dresses and bridesmaids' dresses, too. (Rachelle tells me your bridesmaids will be especially grateful if you choose this option!)

Vegan Shoes

Clothing isn't the only thing we wear on our bodies. You've got to put something on your feet.

As you probably know, most vegans do not wear leather. They avoid leather belts, leather jackets, leather shoes—even leather upholstery on their furniture and in their cars.

My choice to wear vegan shoes (and belts and so on) isn't just about animal cruelty issues. It's also about the environment.

In Chapter 5, "In the Garden and Kitchen," I discussed that it

business. To ensure it remains that way, be sure to spend your dry-cleaning dollars with

takes a lot more land, water, and energy to raise animals than to grow grains and produce. Choosing organic vegan shoes made from plant-based materials is environmentally friendly, too.

Don't assume vegan shoes are much more expensive than other shoes. What did you pay for your last pair of name-brand athletic shoes? My vegan athletic shoes look just the same and they feel the same to me. Any minor difference in cost is a price I'm willing to pay.

A word of caution: You can find inexpensive nonleather shoes, but some of them are not all that well made. There are companies making really cheapo shoes out of plastic because it's less expensive than leather. It's hard for me to find those shoes in my size and in styles that I can tolerate, and when they're badly made, I end up throwing them out after a few months. Plus they're made from petroleum. Any way you look at it, those shoes are a bad investment.

So what are quality vegan shoes made from? In a lot of cases, they're made from hemp, which can look like leather, canvas, even suede. You can also find shoes made from other plant materials, like rubber and jute and cotton. Some vegan shoes even have rubber soles made from recycled car tires. So you can make environmentally friendly choices when it comes to footwear, too.

Dry Cleaning Your Clothes

We covered the benefits of washing your clothes with environmentally friendly detergents in Chapter 1. But what about the stuff that has to be dry cleaned?

Use a Nontoxic Dry Cleaner

COST: Prices are comparable to "traditional" dry cleaners.

The chemical most commonly used in the dry-cleaning process is a solvent called perchloroethylene, or perc. It's considered a toxic air contaminant, and studies have identified it as a carcinogen. It's nasty stuff. Exposure to perc can cause dizziness, headaches, irritation of the eyes and nose and throat, even liver and kidney damage.

merchants who follow eco-friendly practices. **When it comes to buying cosmetics and toiletries,**

Experts will tell you that there's not enough perc on clothing after it's dry cleaned to pose any real danger to you—assuming that the clothing has been aired out properly. It's mostly considered a problem for the people who work in the dry-cleaning industry. On the other hand, do you really want to risk having those chemicals against your skin? And do you really want to encourage the use of this toxic chemical?

RACHELLE'S TURN

I've never liked the smell of clothing that has been dry cleaned. I used to think, "So air it out and it'll be fine." But it's not fine. Perc is a mighty bad toxin and you'll have remnants of it against your skin for ten, maybe twenty hours. Years ago, a town near Boston was found to have a much higher rate of cancer, and it was attributed to the residents' affluent lifestyle, including dry cleaning. They had the money to be exposed to more chemicals.

Fortunately, you can choose where you take your dry cleaning and to give your business to a nontoxic dry cleaner. Some of these cleaners use the practice of *professional wet cleaning*, which is far more environmentally friendly than using perc (and there are other nontoxic options now, too).

I am lucky enough to have one of these nontoxic cleaners within walking distance of my house, and you may, too. It's easy to find out. I'm sure a quick Internet search for your area will turn up choices. For instance, the South Coast Air Quality Management District provides on its website a list of nontoxic dry cleaners in Southern California.

Traditional Skin Care and Hair Care

What you wear isn't the only thing that matters. What you put on your skin and in your hair is important, too.

When you learn what goes into skin- and hair-care products, it's really frightening. So many of the products on the market today—the vast majority of products out there—are full of parabens. According to the U.S. Food and Drug Administration (FDA):

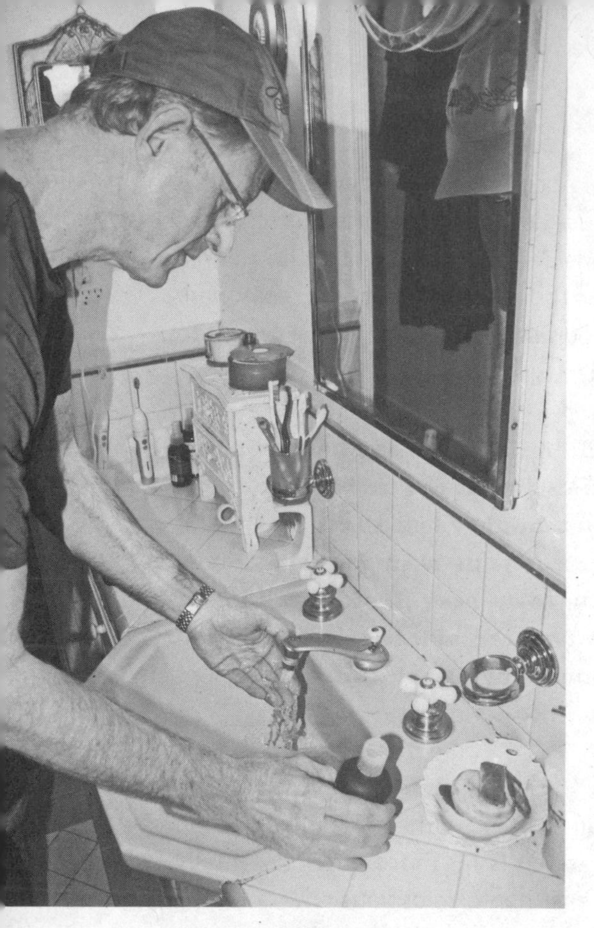

I look for quality, natural, paraben-free products.

"Parabens are the most widely used preservatives in cosmetic products. Chemically, parabens are esters of p-hydroxybenzoic acid. The most common parabens used in cosmetic products are methylparaben, propylparaben, and butylparaben. Typically, more than one paraben is used in a product, and they are often used in combination with other types of preservatives to provide preservation against a broad range of microorganisms."

There's some controversy over parabens. The FDA will tell you the levels used today are safe, but groups like Physicians for Social Responsibility disagree. Parabens mimic estrogen and they've been found—undiluted—in breast cancer tumors. That means these parabens are being absorbed through the skin, because when you eat them, they actually get diluted in your digestive system.

RACHELLE'S TURN

I don't know about you, but I'm not going to risk it. I don't want to use hair- and skin-care products that are full of parabens if I can help it. So many people in my life have been affected by breast cancer, some in their thirties and forties and fifties. It's on the rise, and there's a reason for that.

And parabens are in almost everything on the market. They're in most kinds of shampoo, conditioner, soap, bath gel, facial cleanser and toner, makeup, eye makeup remover, lotion, sunscreen, tanning lotion, and baby lotion, as well as in many other products.

According to the National Institute for Occupational Safety and Health (NIOSH), there are

Beyond that, there's all the petroleum in stuff we use. If you wear lipstick every single day of your life, you eat a pound of petroleum products right there. Petrochemicals are in all sorts of things, from baby oil and Vaseline to anything that says it has paraffin wax as an ingredient.

The more I learn about this stuff, the more I want to learn. You've gotta learn it—and then you've gotta be willing to make changes in your life, because the exposure to these kinds of harmful chemicals is overwhelming, especially in the beauty world.

Organic Skin Care and Hair Care

Rachelle and I have become really attuned to concerns about skin- and hair-care products. We use the best plant-based, natural products that we can. That word *natural* doesn't always have much meaning, but what *I* mean by that is products made with the healthiest materials, products that don't have parabens. Parabens come mostly from fragrances, so I avoid fragrances.

You can find quality, natural, paraben-free products in health food stores. Most hair salons also now offer a complete range of wonderful, natural hair-care products.

RACHELLE'S TURN

Try to stay away from sulfates in hair-care products, too. Sulfates dry your hair out, big-time. Companies add sulfates because they cause sudsing. But suds don't clean hair, and neither do detergents.

My hairstylist, Derek Collins, says the best thing you can do is brush your hair with a boar's-bristle brush every day. This stimulates the scalp and moves the oils away from your scalp and down the hair shaft, where they need to be. It also exfoliates. (Note: If you have hair extensions, I wouldn't suggest this.)

about 36,000 dry cleaning shops in the United States, and about 85 percent of them use

RACHELLE'S TURN

Natural Cosmetics

I love makeup. Eye shadow, mascara, lipstick—all of it. I think putting on makeup is an art form. It can be more dramatic than any outfit you wear. I love trying different products and creating new looks.

Unfortunately, it's been very hard for the natural makeup lines to compete with the premium brands we all swoon over at the department stores. There is not, as yet, sufficient demand for them to hold their own in Macy's and Bloomingdale's, where I usually buy my cosmetics. But I'm putting the extra energy into expanding my shopping expeditions beyond the mall because I'd rather be putting minerals on my skin, as opposed to petroleum-based products. You can find lots of really nice stuff at spas and at stores like Sephora.

Companies are coming out with mineral makeup that offers good sun protection and in colors that Rachelle assures me are appealing and fashionable. Some cosmetics companies have a complete mineral line with everything you'd want, from foundation to eyeliner. Many of these mineral makeup lines are endorsed by doctors—dermatologists and plastic surgeons. That's because this mineral makeup, for the most part, is

- **Hypoallergenic.** It's good for people with sensitive skin, and it tends not to trigger allergic reactions.
- **Breathable.** It feels lighter than traditional base or foundation and it lets your skin breathe. It doesn't clog your pores. Rachelle also says most won't gather in lines and creases and make you look older, either, so there's a real plus!
- **Calming.** Many of the minerals in these products are soothing. Some are even recommended for use after things like laser treatments and chemical peels, when your skin is supersensitive.

perchloroethylene as their primary solvent. Some types of hair dye contain lead acetate.

- **Natural sunblocks.** Zinc oxide, in particular, helps block UVA rays. Remember that white zinc lotion lifeguards would always wear on their noses? You may look a little ghostlike when you wear natural sunblock with zinc oxide in it, but it works, and it's better than all the chemicals in other sunblocks.

You know, you shouldn't have to sacrifice. There are enough talented chemists and visionary company owners out there to create attractive, fashionable cosmetics that are natural, organic, and affordable, too. I'm sure as the demand for these products increases, more companies will invest in research and development.

Reducing Your Exposure to Toxins

Every day, you have the opportunity to be exposed to toxins. You can choose to wear pesticide-laden clothing. You can choose to eat pesticide-laden food. You can choose to wash your hair and your body with products that are full of parabens. Or you can make healthier choices that will also be kinder to the planet.

You can choose to support organic farmers, organic textile companies, organic clothing designers, and organic retailers. You can choose to support natural hair-care and skin-care companies. Even if you have a hard time finding these products locally, let me assure you, they are readily available online.

Just by simply choosing healthful options every day, you can make a world of difference. You can improve your own health and the health of the environment.

It's just like choosing to change your lightbulbs or draw your drapes. Just like choosing to drive a greener car. Just like choosing to recycle and buy recycled. Just like choosing to reduce your energy needs and get your energy from greener sources. Just like choosing to eat locally grown, organic food.

It's all about choices. And you've got the power to choose.

Hair bleach and nail polish may contain formaldehyde.

WORKBOOK

Want to know if this stuff really works? Keep track of just how much money—and energy—you save by making some of the Little Changes, Not-So-Big Changes, and Big Changes outlined in this book. Each time you make a change, record the date you implemented the change. If, for instance, you replace ten incandescent lightbulbs with compact fluorescent lightbulbs (CFLs) or institute a new policy, such as running only full dishwasher or washing machine loads, note the date. When your next utility bill arrives, calculate the difference, and then note which changes were made within that billing period. I bet you will be amazed to see how much it was lowered by making those simple changes.

You'll also find a section for tracking your results. This includes changes in your energy usage as well as health benefits you've noticed, differences in your grocery bills, differences in your gasoline costs, differences in your water usage, and a lot more.

Keeping track of the changes you make and the results in your life is the best way to prove that these changes are good for you *and* good for the environment. After all, the proof is in the savings—and in your improved physical and mental health, too.

CHANGES

ELECTRICITY SAVINGS

Ditch the dirty air filter DATE: _____ COST: _____

Turn down/up the thermostat

I CHANGED THE TEMPERATURE ON MY HEATING SYSTEM FROM:

_____ TO: _____ °F. DATE: _____

I CHANGED THE TEMPERATURE ON MY AIR-CONDITIONING SYSTEM FROM:

_____ °F TO: _____ °F. DATE:

Clean the refrigerator coils DATE: _____

Reseal the refrigerator DATE: _____

COST (FOR MATERIALS AND LABOR, IF APPLICABLE): _____

Reset the refrigerator and freezer settings

I CHANGED THE REFRIGERATOR FROM: _____ °F. TO: _____ °F.

I CHANGED THE FREEZER FROM: _____ °F. TO: _____ °F. DATE: _____

Run only full dishwasher loads DATE: _____

Skip the dishwasher's Heated Dry cycle DATE: _____

Don't prerinse the dishes DATE: _____

Wash only full loads of clothes in cold water

DATE I BEGAN WAITING FOR A FULL LOAD: _____

DATE I SWITCHED TO COLD WATER: _____

Switch to compact fluorescent bulbs (CFLs)

LIGHTBULB CHANGED: _____ DATE: _____ COST: _____

LIGHTBULB CHANGED: _____ DATE: _____ COST: _____

LIGHTBULB CHANGED: _____ DATE: _____ COST: _____

Start turning off appliances, lights, etc. when not in use

DATE: ______

Buy a home energy management system

DATE I INSTALLED THE SYSTEM: ______

COST: ______

Install a net metering setup DATE: ______ COST: ______

Check a box on your electricity bill for green power

PROVIDER: ______

TYPE OF GREEN POWER (E.G., WIND, SMALL HYDROELECTRIC, SOLAR): ______

DATE: ______ COST: ______

Go solar

DATE I INSTALLED A SOLAR ELECTRIC SYSTEM: ______ COST: ______

PERCENT OF MY POWER NEEDS BEING MET BY THE SYSTEM: ______

Lease a solar setup

DATE I INSTALLED A LEASED SOLAR ELECTRIC SYSTEM: ______ COST: ______

PERCENT OF MY POWER NEEDS BEING MET BY THE SYSTEM: ______

Install a wind power system DATE: ______ COST: ______

PERCENT OF MY POWER NEEDS BEING MET BY THE SYSTEM: ______

Install a time-of-use meter DATE: ______ COST: ______

Use power off-peak

AMOUNT OF ENERGY I *USED TO* USE DURING HIGH-PEAK HOURS: ______

DURING LOW-PEAK HOURS: ______ DURING OFF-PEAK HOURS: ______

AMOUNT OF ENERGY I *NOW* USE DURING HIGH-PEAK HOURS: ______

DURING LOW-PEAK HOURS: ______ DURING OFF-PEAK HOURS: ______

ACTIVITIES I'VE BEEN ABLE TO SWITCH TO OFF-PEAK HOURS

____

____

____

____

____

GAS/OTHER ENERGY SAVINGS

Dry clothes on a rack or line DATE: ____ COST: ____

Use the dryer's moisture sensor instead of timed dry

DATE: ____

Clean the dryer's lint filter before each load

DATE: ____

Change the water heater's setting

DATE: ____

I CHANGED IT FROM: ____°F. TO: ____°F.

Wrap the water heater DATE: ____ COST: ____

Draw the drapes

DATE I BEGAN DRAWING THE DRAPES OR CLOSING THE BLINDS OR SHUTTERS AT NIGHT IN THE WINTER: ____

DATE I BEGAN DRAWING THE DRAPES OR CLOSING THE BLINDS OR SHUTTERS DURING THE DAY IN THE SUMMER: ____

Install window film to block UV rays DATE: ____ COST: ____

Caulk around the windows DATE: ____ COST: ____

Install an energy-saving thermostat DATE: _____ COST: _____

Swap a gas mower for an electric or manual model
DATE: _____ COST: _____

Plant a no-mow meadow or lawn DATE: _____ COST: _____

Get a rechargeable leaf blower DATE: _____ COST: _____

Install awnings on south-facing windows (and possibly east- and west-facing windows, too) DATE: _____ COST: _____

Get an Energy Star–qualified air conditioner
DATE: _____ COST: _____

Get a more efficient dishwasher DATE INSTALLED: _____ COST: _____

Get an air purifier DATE: _____ COST: _____

Get an Energy Star–qualified refrigerator
DATE INSTALLED: _____ COST: _____

Get an Energy Star–qualified washing machine
DATE INSTALLED: _____ COST: _____

Add insulation
DATE ADDED TO THE ATTIC: _____ COST: _____
DATE ADDED TO THE WALLS: _____ COST: _____

Get energy-efficient windows
DATE INSTALLED: _____ NUMBER OF WINDOWS CHANGED: _____ COST: _____

Get a highly efficient gas hot water heater

DATE INSTALLED: _____ COST: _____

Let the sun heat your water DATE INSTALLED: _____ COST: _____

WATER SAVINGS

Turn off the tap while brushing teeth, shaving, doing dishes

DATE: _____

Take shorter showers NUMBER OF MINUTES' DIFFERENCE: _____ DATE: _____

Stop hosing off the sidewalk DATE: _____

Take baths instead of showering DATE: _____

Stop flushing your trash DATE: _____

Fix a leaky toilet

DATE: _____ COST (MATERIALS AND LABOR, IF ANY): _____

Get a new low-flow toilet DATE: _____ COST: _____

Water garden/lawns early or late in the day DATE: _____

Do extra watering with a hose or watering can DATE: _____

Buy a rain barrel DATE: _____ COST: _____

Lose the lawn

WHAT IT WAS REPLACED WITH: _____ DATE: _____ COST: _____

RECYCLING CRIB SHEET

Location of my local recycling center

What can go in the curbside recycling bins

What I had been putting in bins by mistake

Closest redemption center or store for returning deposit bottles and cans

Money recouped from redemptions:

DATE: ________ AMOUNT: ________
DATE: ________ AMOUNT: ________
DATE: ________ AMOUNT: ________
DATE: ________ AMOUNT: ________

Location of local recycling center that accepts scrap metal

Items I've recycled so far

Money received/dates

DATE: ____ AMOUNT: ____

DATE: ____ AMOUNT: ____

DATE: ____ AMOUNT: ____

DATE: ____ AMOUNT: ____

Avoid products packaged in no. 3 and no. 5 plastics

ITEMS I USUALLY BUY THAT COME IN NO. 3 AND NO. 5 PLASTICS	AVAILABLE IN ALTERNATIVE PACKAGING?	COST DIFFERENTIAL

Location of my local recycling center

Location of a cleaner or grocery that accepts plastic bags

MONEY RECEIVED/DATES

DATE: ______________ AMOUNT: ______________

DATE: ______________ AMOUNT: ______________

DATE: ______________ AMOUNT: ______________

DATE: ______________ AMOUNT: ______________

DATE: ______________ AMOUNT: ______________

Location of special recycling center for high-quality paper

____

____

MONEY RECEIVED/DATES

DATE: ______________ AMOUNT: ______________

DATE: ______________ AMOUNT: ______________

DATE: ______________ AMOUNT: ______________

DATE: ______________ AMOUNT: ______________

DATE: ______________ AMOUNT: ______________

Donate magazines after reading them

LOCATIONS AT WHICH I'VE DONATED MAGAZINES	DATE	NUMBER/VALUE OF MAGAZINES
TOTAL TAX WRITE-OFF: ______		

Location of my local hazardous waste drop-off center

____

____

Items I've dropped off

Location of drop-off center for partially filled paint cans

Location of my local computer recycling center

Items I've dropped off

Location of my local thrift shop or other drop-off centers

ITEMS DONATED	DATE	VALUE
TOTAL TAX WRITE-OFF: ______		

Location of my local eyeglass drop-off center

______

Location of my local cell phone drop-off center

______

TOTAL TAX WRITE-OFF: ______

RESULTS

ELECTRIC BILLS

The best way to get a feel for how much energy—and money—you're saving is to compare your energy bills. Specifically, you'll want to compare the year-to-year bills (i.e., the April 2008 bill against the April 2007 bill) to minimize the differences in seasonal usage.

Here's a chart that makes it easy for you to record your electric bills. First write down the amount of each of your electric bills over the last year (e.g., April 2007, May 2007, June 2007, etc.). Continue to record the amount of your electric bill each month as it arrives. Then subtract the recent bill's total from the previous year's to get a sense of your savings, and just how much of a difference all of these Easy, Not-So-Big, and Big Changes have made in your energy consumption.

Since your utility company may increase its rates over time, I've included a space to record the number of kilowatt-hours you've used. This kilowatt-hour information is also handy to have when you want to purchase a TerraPass or other carbon offset product, or whenever you decide to look into a wind or solar electric system for your home.

MONTH	NO. OF KILOWATT-HOURS USED	ELECTRIC BILL AMOUNT

MONTH	NO. OF KILOWATT-HOURS USED	ELECTRIC BILL AMOUNT

GAS BILLS

Just as you've recorded your electric bills, you'll also want to keep track of your natural gas bills, so you can appreciate those energy savings.

Again, start by writing down the amount of each of your monthly, bimonthly, or quarterly gas bills over the last year. Then continue recording the amount of your gas bill each month as it arrives.

Many gas bills include information on daily average use, which is a good way to keep track of your energy use over time. If your bill does not have this feature, you can record the number of therms used or whatever quantity/usage figure your utility company provides.

MONTH	DAILY AVERAGE USE	GAS BILL AMOUNT

MONTH	DAILY AVERAGE USE	GAS BILL AMOUNT

WATER BILLS

Many of the changes we've discussed will cut back on your water usage. This chart provides an easy place to record your water bills, so you can see the difference you've made.

MONTH	WATER USAGE	WATER BILL AMOUNT

GASOLINE COSTS

Many of the transportation changes we discussed in Chapter 2 will affect your gasoline costs, and so will some of the garden-related changes, such as switching from a gasoline-powered lawn mower to a push mower or an electric mower. Here's the place to keep track of your gasoline expenses over time.

MONTH	GALLONS USED	GASOLINE COSTS

HEALTH BENEFITS

A lot of the changes you've been making will have health benefits. Here's a handy place to keep track of the benefits you've seen. In each case, just record the action you've taken and then record any benefits you've experienced.

For instance, if you start riding your bike to work, you might notice increased muscle tone, better stamina, and feeling more relaxed overall. Or if you switch to earth-friendly paints, you might notice that you and your family experience fewer headaches, fewer allergies, less sniffling, and so on.

To help get you started, I've filled in a few of the actions here.

ACTION I'VE TAKEN	HEALTH BENEFITS I'VE NOTICED
Switched to earth-friendly cleaners	
Used nontoxic paint	
Aired out my home	
Purchased an air purifier	
Began walking to restaurants	
Begin riding my bike to work	
Took up gardening	
Cleansed my body of toxins	
Began eating more slowly	

RECYCLING-RELATED BENEFITS

When you start recycling on a regular basis, you'll notice a real difference in the amount of trash you're sending to a landfill. It might be fun—and revealing—to keep track of just how full your trash cans are or how many bags you put out for pickup, as you begin getting into the recycling routine.

Perhaps you normally fill up two trash cans each week. Over time, you might fill just one can per week, or perhaps it will only be half full.

MONTH	AMOUNT OF TRASH IN MY TRASH CANS(S)

You also might notice some other benefits from the various types of recycling we discussed, like giving stuff away to charity, using a service like Freecycle, or holding a garage sale. Here's a place to record those benefits.

Any extra room in my garage or closets or elsewhere? ______
Any psychological relief from reduced clutter? ______

CHARITY-RELATED BENEFITS

If you donate items to charity—including things like clothes, linens, toys, computers, cell phones, and books—you typically will get a tax write-off. Here's a handy place to keep track of what you've donated and the financial benefit you've received.

DATE OF DONATION	ITEMS DONATED	CHARITY THAT BENEFITS	ESTIMATED VALUE FOR TAX WRITE-OFF

GROCERY BILLS

When you grow your own food, you should see some real savings on your grocery bill.

MONTH	GROCERY COSTS

YARD-CARE COSTS

If you've made some of the other garden-related changes we've discussed, such as removing or reducing the size of your lawn or changing from needy plants to native ones, you may see some real savings in your yard-care costs. For instance, you might be paying less for yard and garden maintenance. If you've been making your own compost and using it throughout your yard, you might be spending less on fertilizer and weed-control products. And if you've stopped buying poisons and you've started buying beneficial insects, you should see some cost savings there as well.

Here's a good place to track your yard-care costs over time.

MONTH	YARD-CARE COSTS

STILL MORE RESULTS

Many other changes can yield all kinds of great results. For example, if you've gotten your kids involved in gardening, they may have learned about the cycle of life or about where food comes from. They might even have developed an interest in cooking.

If you've switched from paying your bills by mail to paying them online, you've certainly saved on postage costs, and you might even have saved several trips to the post office, which can save time and gasoline.

Likewise, if you've switched from sending letters to doing more of your correspondence by e-mail, you'll save stamps and paper and envelopes.

Switching from disposable batteries to rechargeable ones can mean money in your pocket and fewer trips to the store, too.

You also might have noticed some other benefits if you've started growing your own food or buying organic meat and produce at a store or a farmers' market. For instance, there could be an obvious difference in the quality of the meat and produce, or in the flavors—even in how long produce lasts once you've purchased it. You also may feel an enhanced sense of community.

This chart is a great place to record these results—and others—that you've noticed as you've made lifestyle changes. Again, I've filled in a few examples to get you going.

ACTION I'VE TAKEN	BENEFITS I'VE NOTICED
Got the kids involved in gardening	
Paid bills online	
Sent e-mails instead of letters	
Switched to rechargeable batteries	
Switched to organic meat	
Switched to organic produce	
Began shopping at a farmers' market	

ACTION I'VE TAKEN	BENEFITS I'VE NOTICED

THE BOTTOM LINE

By now, I'm sure you've proved to yourself—and perhaps a doubting spouse or friend—that making environmentally friendly choices is good not just for the environment, it's good for your pocketbook, too.

ACKNOWLEDGMENTS

Sue Elliott—Thank you for being my writing partner.

David Brower—You are a constant source of inspiration for me.

Gavin De Becker—Thank you for giving me confidence as an author.

Joe Brutsman—Thank you for creating *Living with Ed.*

Bud Brutsman, Jen Shields, Andy Robinson, Brooke Murdock, Kellie Weston, and the *Living with Ed* BCII Production Team—Thank you.

Greg Glass—Thank you for the work.

INDEX